SUNDAY SCHOOLS AND WOMEN'S FELLOWSHIPS IN ALL CHURCHES

Dr. Manohar Rao in front of the Holy Cross Cathedral

About 200 boys attending Sunday School

About 200 girls attending Sunday School

SUNDAY SCHOOLS AND WOMEN'S FELLOWSHIPS IN ALL CHURCHES

P.J. Manohar Rao (Dr.)
and
P.J. Pancharatnam (Rev. Dr.)

Foreword by
Ashish Amos (Rev. Dr.)
General Secretary, ISPCK

ISPCK
2009

SUNDAY SCHOOLS AND WOMEN'S FELLOWSHIPS IN ALL CHURCHES – Published by the Rev. Dr. Ashish Amos of the Indian Society for Promoting Christian Knowledge (ISPCK), Post Box 1585, 1654, Madarsa Road, Kashmere Gate, Delhi-110006.

Dr. P.J. Manohar Rao,
A-101, Yamuna Apartments,
Alaknanda,
New Delhi-110 019
Ph.: 0 9818113420
   (011) 40533 455, 26001581

Rev. Dr. P.J. Pancharatnam,
P.O.: Nandyal, R.S.
Dist. Kurnool - 518 502
Andhra Pradesh
Ph.: 0 9948111375
   (08514) 248513

ISBN: 978-81-8465-019-8

Laser typeset by **ISPCK,** Post Box, 1585, 1654, Madarsa Road, Kashmere Gate, Delhi-110006.
Tel: 23866323/22
e-mail– ashish@ispck.org.in • ella@ispck.org.in
website-www.ispck.org.in

Contents

1.
Foreword

Since Sunday Schools are citadels of Christian nurture for our children and women's fellowships are the bastions of family values inculcated through our church going women who manage our homes, hence it is important for us to provide the full meaning of the Christian faith and scriptures to both our children and women. In times of struggles as these it is an effort to help them to hold on to God no matter what.

The purpose of this book is to help Christians grasp the basic meaning, of the Christian doctrines, traditions and events so that the act of praying might truly become an elevation of the mind to God. After providing general background on biblical teachings P.J. Manohar Rao offers the lay perspective to important events and tradition of the Church. He avoids exegetical minutiae, providing instead precisely enough explanation of the original cultural and theological setting of each important event or tradition in a separate chapter to let the usefulness of understanding them fully emerge.

A widely respected Christian scholar Dr. P.J. Manohar Rao has authored several general and Christian books significant among these being "Walking with Jesus in the Holy Land."

As a result his book not only offers learned insight into the meaning of important Christian traditions but is also built on personal experiences making it a powerful learning tool.

After studying the working of the Sunday Schools and Women's Fellowships in different churches, he has now chosen to write about these two important activities of every church. He had actually developed the Sunday School of the Holy Cross Cathedral, Nandyal (A.P.) which is his home town, by providing biblical pictures, books, DVDs etc. purchased from ISPCK, as there are as many as 500 children attending the Sunday School of the Cathedral. He also addressed the Women's Fellowship attached to this Cathedral many times and guided them on the ways and means of improving its working so that it may be really useful to the entire congregation and communities around the Cathedral. It is a fact that the members of the Women's Fellowships, who are mostly mothers, are the teachers of the Sunday School children, when the children are at home. So, both the teachers of Sunday school, as well as the mothers must have a thorough knowledge of the entire Bible, particularly the interesting stories, parables, miracles performed by our Lord and Saviour Jesus Christ, so that they can narrate these to the children.

As the Holy Bible is voluminous with 39 books in the Old Testament and 27 books in the New Testament, it is rather difficult to immediately locate any particular instance in the Bible. So, to make it easy, Dr. Rao has prepared separate chapters for; i) Contents of each of the 66 books in the Holy Bible, ii) Stories in the Holy Bible, iii) Parables in the Bible, iv) Miracles in the Bible and special subjects like Ark of the Covenant, Ten Commandments, Sabbath day, Crucifixion of Jesus Christ, Fourteen Stations of the Cross (Via-Dolorosa) etc.

Readers will find here helpful portions for living and engaging the gospel in today's troubled world.

Rev. Dr. Ashish Amos

2.
Preface

Dr. P.J. Manohar Rao,
New Delhi

Rev. Dr. P.J. Pancharatnam,
Nandyal (A.P.)

Dr. P. J. Manohar Rao and his younger brother, Rev. Dr. P. J. Pancharatnam are from Nandyal (A.P.) They are members of the Holy Cross Cathedral, Nandyal. They are closely associated with all activities of this Cathedral for the last 70 years. A brief of them is on the back cover of this book.

Dr. Manohar Rao, wrote many technical books, which were published by ISPCK, New Delhi. His prestigious book is "Walking with Jesus in the Holy Land", which he wrote after visiting the Holy Land in the year 2006. It is a pictorial narrative and highly appreciated by all readers including clergy. Appreciating the contents of this book, he was awarded two Doctorates simultaneously – one from a Theological College in California (USA) and another from the Gurukul Theological College, Chennai.

Dr. Pancharatnam also wrote many books like "Synoptic Gospels", "Early Christians", "Maha Yagna" etc. Two of these books were published by ISPCK, New Delhi. Thus, both are veteran authors of books.

After studying the Sunday Schools and Women's Fellowships in different churches in Andhra Pradesh, New Delhi, Mumbai, Chennai, etc, a need was felt to guide the Sunday School teachers, and members of the Women's Fellowships in a better way. They hope that this book will be helpful to all.

"MAY OUR LORD AND SAVIOUR JESUS CHRIST BLESS YOU ALL ABUNDANTLY."

Dr. Manohar Rao

&

Rev. Dr. Pancharatnam

3.
Introduction
Sunday Schools and Women's Fellowship

The churches in all countries have many activities for the benefit of the congregational members, their families, children and surrounding communities, in addition to conducting regular prayer services, religious meetings etc. Of all these activities, conducting Sunday Schools for the Children and Women's Fellowships are very important and these two are inter-connected. The reason is that in a Sunday School, the children are taught by the Sunday School teachers, whereas at home, their mothers, who are also members of the Women's Fellowship, are their teachers throughout the twenty-four hours. Thus, at home, the mothers who are members of the Women's Fellowship play the role of Sunday School teachers for the children.

Children are special gifts of God to humanity and nation. Psalm 127: 3 in the Holy Bible says, "Sons are a heritage from the Lord, children a reward from him." The greatest gift that the parents can give to their children in return to the God's gift is to develop in children faith in our Lord and Saviour Jesus Christ from their childhood. As children are free from worldly worries and anxieties like elders, their minds are fresh to understand anything that is taught to them in childhood and remember it throughout their lives. Mother's teaching particularly is imbedded in the minds of young children and even in their old age also, they say, "My mother said like this etc." The little girls who are taught by their mothers, when they become mothers in the later years, repeat to their children, the same things which they learnt from their mothers and thus, from generation to generation, the knowledge is transferred. The elders have to first learn and understand the entire Holy Bible and then pass on their knowledge to their youngsters and so on.

The Lord said (Deuteronomy 4:1), "Hear now O Israel, the decrees and laws I am about to teach you. Follow them."

In Deuteronomy 6:4 to 7, it is said, "Hear, O Israel, : The Lord our God, is one Lord. And thou shalt love the Lord thy God with all thine heart, and with all thy soul, and with all thy might. And these words, which I command thee this day, shall be, in thine heart : And thou shalt teach them diligently unto thy children, and shalt talk of them, when thou sittest in thine house, and when thou walkest by the way, and when thou liest down, and when thou riseth up."

Again in Deuteronomy 11:19, it is said "Teach my words to your children, talking about them when you sit at home, and when you walk along them on the road, when you lie down and when you get up." Thus, our Lord God said that the elders must teach the children throughout the day, when they are with the children.

Proverbs 22:6 says, "Train a child in the way he should go, and when he is old, he will not turn from it."

So, it is the responsibility of the Sunday School teachers and mothers, who are all members of the Women's Fellowship to bring up the Christian children in the fear of the Lord and Saviour Jesus Christ from their young age, so that the children in their turn when they grow up, repeat the same with the children of that time.

3-A : SUNDAY SCHOOLS

Nearly 228 years ago, in the year 1780, Robert Rakes of England started Sunday School for the children, in order to give a good knowledge of the Holy Bible to all Christian children. Later on, William Fox and John Wesley started Sunday Schools on the 7th September, 1785. So, 7th September of every year is celebrated in all churches in the World as "World Sunday School Day."

1. TIMING OF SUNDAY SCHOOL CLASSES

From very old times, in all the churches, Sunday School classes are conducted simultaneously in an adjoining hall while the Sunday services are held in the church. This practice is mainly due to the reason that in almost all cities and in some towns, the congregational members stay far away from the churches and it is safe for their children to accompany the parents while coming to the Sunday School and go along with them after the Sunday School Classes are over. So, the Sunday School classes and the Sunday service have to be conducted simultaneously in two separate buildings. But, in many villages and some towns, the congregational members reside within walking distance from the church. In such places, Sunday School classes are held at any convenient time for the children, usually in the afternoons, as the children can walk up on their own to the church compound to attend the Sunday School classes and go back on their own.

In some churches, the elders are of the opinion that the children also should attend the Sunday service in the church at least for some time, so that they get knowledge of the service also from their childhood. So, in many churches, the children sit in the church service till the sermon begins and then go to the Sunday School classes. In this case, the children do not get sufficient time to learn a lot in the Sunday School class, as they have to leave in the middle of the class to go home along with their parents. But, in case the children attend the class as soon as the service starts in the church, they will have a fairly good time to learn a lot in the class. If the Sunday School classes are conducted at different times and the children come and go without accompanying their parents, the children get lot of time to learn a lot in the Sunday School Class.

Whatever may be the timing of Sunday School classes, the main idea is to ensure adequate time for the children to learn a lot about the Holy Bible in the Sunday School classes.

2.　AGE WISE GROUPING OF SUNDAY SCHOOL CHILDREN

It is very well known that the intellectual calibre and grasping capacity of the children depend on the age of the children. Very young children usually love to hear stories and when the beautiful stories in the Holy Bible are narrated to them, the stories are fixed in their little and sharp brains and they remember them for ever. The young children look forward to every Sunday to attend the Sunday School class and hear the stories. Thus, from childhood, they become lovers of Sunday School classes. As the children grow up, their taste of stories also get changed and they love to hear stories of horror, fighting, thrill, etc., instead of fairly tales. There are many interesting stories of different types in the Holy Bible to suit the taste of children of different age groups. It is for the Sunday School teachers to select most suitable stories from the Holy Bible for children of different age groups.

A survey of Sunday schools conducted in different churches has indicated that the usual grouping of the children according to their age is as follows:-

i)	Beginners	–	Ages 4,5 and 6 years.
ii)	Primary	–	Ages 7,8 and 9 years.
iii)	Junior	–	Ages 10,11 and 12 years.
iv)	Intermediate	–	Ages 13,14 and 15 years.
v)	Senior	–	Ages 16,17 and 18 years.

However, this age grouping can be altered depending on local circumstances.

SYLLABUS FOR EACH AGE GROUP CHILDREN

By and large, there is no particular syllabus prescribed by any organization for the Sunday School children of different age groups. Normally, the Sunday School superintendent, in consultation with all the Sunday School teachers, prepare the syllabus for children of different age groups for the entire year. Whatever may be the syllabus followed by Sunday Schools in different areas, their main concentration should be on the Holy Bible.

However, the following organizations guide all Sunday Schools, by providing suitable syllabus for children of different age groups :-

i)   All India Sunday School Association
     Plot No.: 8,
     Road No.: 16,
     Threemurthy Colony,
     Mahendra Hills,
     SECUNDERABAD – 500 026, A.P.
     Phone (040)27737576

ii) CEEFI Supply Centre Trust
     4-1-826, J.N.Road,
     Victoria Chambers,
     HYDERABAD – 500 001, A.P.
     Phone (040)24605194

iii) CEEFI Telugu
     1-1-2/D, Jawahar Nagar,
     RTC Cross Roads,
     Besides Telephone Exchange,
     HYDERABAD – 500 020, A.P.
     Phone (040) 27615952

iv) India Sunday School Union
Keswick,
Orange Groove Road,
COONOR – 643101
Tamilnadu.
Phone (0423) 2230476

v) Vacation Bible School Ministries
No. 3 – Norris Road,
Richmond Town,
BANGALORE – 560 025

vi) General Secretary
Church of South India,
CSI Centre,
No. 5, Whites Road,
Royapettah,
CHENNAI - 600 014

All the Sundays Schools can write to the above organizations and get guidance from time to time.

As the entire emphasis of teaching in the Sunday Schools should be on the Holy Bible, it is very important for the Sunday School teachers to be thorough with the contents of the Holy Bible. The above organizations insist on the proper training of the Sunday School teachers, by giving them opportunity to participate in any training programmes organized by different churches or institutions or revival meetings, etc.

The Sunday School teachers should have a good idea of the contents of the 39 books in the Old Testament and 27 books in the New Testament, the Miracles, Parables and various subjects of interest to the children. But, the Bible is voluminous with 66 books and some books running into many pages. The Old Testament contains the names of many places and people, which are not very essential for the young children. When they grow up, they will be able to go through the entire Holy Bible more than once and get knowledge of these places, etc. Therefore, for easy and quick reference of the Sunday School teachers, members of the Women's Fellowships, and even Sunday School children, an effort has been made in this book, to prepare separate chapters as follows: -

1. Brief contents of the 39 books of the Old Testament.
2. Brief contents of the 27 books of the New Testament.
3. Important stories of the Old Testament.
4. Important stories of the New Testament.
5. Parables in the Old Testament, in serial order.
6. Miracles in the Old Testament, in serial order.
7. Parables in the New Testament, in serial order.
8. Miracles in the New Testament, in serial order.
9. Miracles in the Act of Apostles, Epistles of Paul, and Revelations.
10. Ark of the Covenant, Tabernacle and other items of worship, as commanded by Lord God to Moses on Mount Sinai.
11. Ten Commandments, as written by Lord with his own hand on two tablets of stone and given to Moses.
12. Observance of Sabbath Day.
13. Crucifixion of Jesus Christ, Seven Words spoken by Jesus Christ from the Cross, Resurrection and Ascension of Jesus Christ to Heaven.
14. Fourteen Stations of the Cross (via Dolorosa).

Thus, there is such a lot of interesting material in the Holy Bible to be taught to the Sunday School children of different age groups.

Occasionally, Bible Quiz can be organized to encourage the Sunday School children to brush up their knowledge of the Holy Bible and get through the competition. By offering a small gift for the winner, the children will be more interested in participating in the competition and thus, their knowledge of the Holy Bible gradually increase.

There are many interesting stories in the Holy Bible. The children can be trained to enact some of these stories. Usually, in all the churches, the Sunday School children are trained to enact the "Nativity Play" during the Christmas season. But, there are many more interesting stories like, i) David and Goliath, ii) Samson and Delilah, iii) Joseph in Egypt, iv) Daniel, Shadrach, Meshach and Abednego, etc. in the Old Testament, and i) The Prodigal son, ii) Good Samaritan, iii) Conversion of Saul on the way to Damascus, etc. in the New Testament. Some of stories can be enacted by the Sunday School children, if they are properly trained with suitable costumes, etc. Usually, all children are interested in enacting some drama or the other. By this, the Sunday School children will remember the story and dialogues for a long time in their life and try to train the younger generations also in similar activities.

Similarly, the Sunday School children should be taught different Christian songs and lyrics. Dances by singing christian songs also should be taught to the children.

Organizing Inter-Sunday School competitions now and then in the form of quiz, dramas, songs and dances will encourage the Sunday School children of all the nearby churches to participate in these competitions to win prizes etc.

Children should memorize the Lord's Prayer, Psalms 23, 91, etc.

NEED TO HAVE A LIBRARY IN THE SUNDAY SCHOOL

In order to impart good knowledge of the Bible to the Sunday School teachers, as well as its students, it is very essential to have a small library in every Sunday School. For the knowledge of the Sunday School teachers, a few copies of the Holy Bible, the New Testaments, lyric books, different Bible storybooks, magazines, sermons, commentaries, etc. should be kept in the

Sunday Schools library. The children love to go through pictorial storybooks, as they grasp the stories better by looking into the relevant pictures. Now and then, the pictorial story books should be given to the little children so that, they may go through them and understand the story told to them.

The hall in which the Sunday School classes are conducted should have many biblical pictures fixed on the walls. Every Sunday, a group of children may be made to sit in front of a particular picture and the story in the picture explained to them. Thus, by rotation, different age group children can be taught about different pictures. For the sake of senior children, maps of, i) Palestine in Jesus' days, ii) Moses leading the Israelites for 40 years from Egypt to Canaan, iii) Jerusalem in Jesus Christ's days and at present, iv) The conquest of Canaan by Israelites, v) Paul's first and second journeys (Acts 13 and 14; 15:39:18:22), vi) Paul's third and fourth journeys (Acts 18:23; 21:16; 27 and 28:16) etc. should be fixed on the walls, and the senior children should be made to study them carefully.

If funds are available for the Sunday Schools, children should be given pictorial pamphlets of the biblical stories. Similarly, outline drawings of the biblical pictures should be given to little children and they are made to colour them suitably, at home.

Biblical books, storybooks, pamphlets, maps etc. can be procured from the following firms :-

1.	Christian Literature Society (CLS)
	Park Town,
	Evening Bazaar Road,
	CHENNAI – 600 001
	Ph.: (044) 25354296,
		(044) 25354297

2. ISPCK Book Publishers abd Distributors,
   1654, Madarsa Road,
   Kashmere Gate,
   DELHI – 110 006
   Phone: (011) 23866323/22

3. Bible Society of India,
   "Logos",
   26, Mahatma Gandhi Road,
   BANGALORE – 560 001
   Phone: (080) 41124714

4. Alfa Book Centre,
   Alphine Road,
   Dwaraka Nagar,
   VISHAKHAPATNAM – 530 016
   A.P.
   Phone: (0891) 2501513

5. Motive Books Ltd.,
   B – 124, Jangpura – B
   NEW DELHI – 110 014
   Phone: (011) 65860009

6. OM Books, "LOGOS BHAVAN",
   Jeedimetla Village,
   Medichal Road,
   SECUNDERABAD – 500 055
   A.P.
   Phone: (040) 7860449, (040) 7863188

7. Shri. P.B.Manohar,
   10-10-57 Chenchupeta,
   TENALI – 522 202
   Dist. Guntur
   A.P.
   Phone : 9848363638

8. Tiny Tot Publications,
    235 – Jagriti Enclave,
    Vikas Marg,
    DELHI – 110 092
    Phone: (011) 22167314

All the books, maps, etc. should be properly numbered and arranged in a cupboard.

As children like to go through pictorial books, they also like to watch the television, when a biblical programme is televised, as they like cartoon pictures. Now a days, many DVDs with biblical stories and cartoon are available. If funds permit or a generous member of the congregation or any one else is able to donate, it will be an excellent idea to purchase a TV, with biblical DVDs and shown to the Sunday School children now and then. This will increase the knowledge of the children very much. This will also attract more children to attend Sunday School classes.

HOW SHOULD THE SUNDAY SCHOOL CHILDREN BEHAVE

St. Paul the apostle, in his letter to Ephesians wrote (Eph. 6:1 to 4) "Children, obey your parents in the Lord, for this is right. Honour thy father and mother: (which is the first commandment with promise). That it may be well with thee, and thou mayest live long on the earth."

As quoted earlier, Proverbs of King Solomon (the son of King David), mentioned (Pro. 22:6) "Train up a child in the way he should go: and when he is old, he will not depart from it."

All the Sunday School children should keep the above in their mind and respect their parents and all elders. They should be very regular and punctual to attend the Sunday School classes every Sunday. They should complete any home work given by the Sunday School teacher on the previous Sunday.

The homework may be of any type like, painting a picture, writing a biblical story, answering biblical questions, etc. The children should try to spend more time in the Sunday School class to learn as much as possible from the Bible or Christian songs, learn dramas, etc.

At home, they should try to read a small portion of the Bible every morning before they start any work or studies, meditate and pray to our Lord and Saviour Jesus Christ for his blessings and protecting them in whatever they do during the day. By following all these principles, they will receive the abundant blessings of Jesus Christ and shine in all their activities in the school, colleges and jobs when they grow up as adults.

3-B: WOMEN'S FELLOWSHIP

The term "Women's Fellowship" is a general term used in almost all the churches. In the earlier years, this was known as "Women's Union", and "Mother's Union." Later on, it was felt that in addition to all mothers, other women could also join as members. So, it was known as "Women's Fellowship" to represent an organization of all women in a church. But, in different states of India, many local names are used, such as "Sthreela Maitri", etc.

By and large, in all Women's Fellowships of different churches, the main objectives of these groups are as follows: -

1. To bring up the children in a God fearing manner from a very young age. The Holy Bible says that Timothy was taught by his mother and grandmother. Paul, an apostle of Jesus Christ in his epistle to Timothy (II Timothy 1:5) said "When I call to remembrance, the unfeigned faith that is in thee, which dwelt first in thy grand mother Lois, and thy mother Eunice: and I am persuaded that in thee also."

2. To impart a good knowledge of the Holy Bible to the children depending on their age, by way of telling the Bible stories, which the children usually love and can easily grasp and retain in their little minds.

3. Make the children acquire good manners and respect for parents and all elders. Jesus Christ said, "Honour thy father and mother. (Matthew 19:19).

4. Make the children read a portion of the Holy Bible every morning, meditate for a while and pray to our Lord and Saviour Jesus Christ, before they start their day-to-day studies and other work.

    In II Timothy 3:15, it is said, "And that from a child thou hast known the Holy Scriptures, which are able to make thee wise unto salvation through faith, which is Christ Jesus." Bible reading is the most important duty of every Christian. Writings of the Holy Bible was inspired by God (II Timothy 3:16). So, when you are reading the Holy Bible, you are actually reading the words of God himself.

Prayer is also very important. Jesus Christ himself said (Luke 18:1), "Men ought always to pray and not to faint." Paul, the apostle of Jesus Christ, in his First Epistle to Timothy, chapter 2:8 said, "I will, therefore, that men pray everywhere lifting up holy hands, without wrath and doubting."

Jesus Christ was also praying to His Father in Heaven many times, sometimes in loneliness and sometimes prayed the whole night. Jesus Christ taught his disciples also a simple prayer, which is now known as the "Lord's Prayer", which is frequently used by all christians, now a days (Luke 11:1 to 4).

Jesus Christ said (Matthew 6:6), "When thou prayest, enter into thy closet and when hast shut the door, pray to thy Father, which is in secret : and thy Father which seeth in secret shall reward thee openly."

5. Make the children attend the church service every morning and evening, if the church is located nearby or at least on every Sunday, if the church is located far away and make the children attend the Sunday School classes regularly to learn more about our Lord and Saviour, Jesus Christ.

6. Induce and encourage the children to take an active part in all the activities of the church and Sunday School.

7. The Women should develop harmonius atmosphere in the family, so that all the members of the family live in happiness and in a God fearing manner always.

Paul, an apostle of Jesus Christ, in his Epistle to Titus (Chapter 2:1 to 4) said, "Speak thou the things, which become sound doctrine. That the aged men be sober, grave, temperate, sound in faith, in charity and in patience. The aged women likewise, that they be in behaviour as becometh holiness, not false accusers, not given to much wine, teachers of good things. That they may teach the young women to be sober, to love their husbands, to love their children. To be discreet, chaste, keepers at home good, obedient to their husbands, that the word of God be not blasphemed."

8. Women should counsel all the members of the family suitably and with constant prayers to mend any member of the family going astray and leading a sinful life.

9. Women should cultivate the habit of conducting family prayers regularly every morning and evening, depending on the convenience of all the members of the family.

10. Women should cultivate among the family members, the habit of praying before beginning anything, pray before every meal, pray if any one is sick and in trouble.

11. Women should counsel alcoholics, drug addicts, smokers, law breakers, religious fanatics, trouble creators, rowdies, juvenile offenders, and pray for them and make them refrain from all such bad habits and become God's children.

12. Groups of women should regularly visit ailing members of the congregation, patients in the hospitals, and render all kinds of help possible and encourage them by prayers for their speedy recovery. If there are a few members in the Women's Fellowship from medical profession, like nursing sisters, midwives, doctors, etc., they can be formed into a "Health Visitors" group and regularly visit the sick people. This will be a great help and encouragement to any ailing members of the congregation.

In general, Epistle of James addressed to the Jewish converts, who were living outside the Holy Land, James said (Chapter 5:14 and 15), "If anyone is sick among you, let him call for the elders of the church, and let them pray over him, anointing him with oil in the name of the Lord. And the prayers of the faith shall save the sick, and the Lord shall raise him up: and if he has committed sins, they shall be forgiven him."

13. The Women should look after the poor widows, destitutes, and socially depressed people and render all possible help.

14. Women should promote love and affection among all the members of the congregation, so that they all can live like a single family in happiness.

    A simple sentence of our Lord and Saviour Jesus Christ "Love thy neighbour as thyself" (Matthew 19:19) covers the entire field of the need to love one another and live in peace. Jesus Christ again said (John 13:34 and 35), "A new commandment I give unto you, that ye love one another. By this, shall all men know that ye are my disciples if ye have love one to another."

    In the First Epistle of Paul to Corinthians, Paul said (Chapter 13:13), "And now abideth faith, hope and love these three, but the greatest of these is love."

15. Women should visit the prisoners in jails occasionally, at least on Christian festival days, with some gifts, read the Bible verses to them and counsel them to lead a better life in future.

16. For enabling the women of the Women's Fellowship to carry out all the above activities and many more, they require sufficient funds. In addition to their own contributions, funds from the church and any donations from generous members of the congregation, the women themselves should start small projects for raising funds.

For instance, for over 100 years, a simple scheme known as "Handful of Rice Scheme" is prevalent in all the North-Eastern States of India, like Meghalaya, Mizoram, Nagaland, Tripura, etc., for raising funds for the Women's Fellowships. According to this scheme, all Christian women keep aside a handful of rice before they cook a meal. Rich women may keep aside more rice than mere handful. At the end of every week, church volunteers collect rice from all families and sell it to needy families at a slightly lower price than the market price. The funds so generated are used for meeting the expenditure of Women's Fellowship or any other church activity.

In different churches of India, the Women's Fellowships have introduced different activities to raise fund. In some churches, the women sell cookies, coffee, tea, knitware, Christmas cards, biblical pictures, cassettes of Christian lyrics and songs, spices, etc. for raising funds. Sometimes, the women purchase eatable from shops and bakeries and sell them at a slightly higher price. All these activities are carried out outside the church and after the service is over.

The Holy Bible mentions about many women noted for their outstanding characteristics, which the present day women should try to follow. For instance, I Samuel 1:10 to 28 says that Eli was the priest in the temple. Elkanath had two wives. One was Hanna. She had no children. She was constantly praying to the Lord weeping and saying "O Lord, if you show mercy on me and bless me with a male child, then I will give him to you the days of his life." Priest Eli blessed her by saying that God will grant her petition. Accordingly, Hanna was blessed with a son, and named him Samuel. When the child grew up, Hanna took him to the temple and lent him to the Lord to serve him as long as he lived.

I Samuel 3:4 to 11 says that the Lord called him (Samuel) thrice one night. But, Samuel thought it was Eli calling him and Samuel went to Eli. But, Eli said that it was not he who was calling, but the Lord. The Lord appeared to Samuel and spoke to him. Samuel served the Lord throughout his life. Thus, Hanna, the mother of Samuel offered her son's services to the Lord throughout his lifetime, as she vowed to the Lord.

There are many other notable women mentioned in the Holy Bible. Women should read all these and explain to the children.

It is the duty of parents, particularly the mothers to teach all about the Holy Bible, all the stories, parables, and miracles in it to the children. It is very well known to all that "Mother is the best teacher of her child." Whatever mothers tell their children, they always remember it throughout their life. Some times they proudly tell others what their mothers told them. So, mother has a major role in molding the behaviour, knowledge, and habits of their children. As all the mothers are members of the Women's Fellowship, it is important for them to teach their children and make them understand all the contents of the Holy Bible, depending on the age of the children.

All the children are fond of hearing stories, particularly before they sleep in the bed with their mother by their side. That is why, many stories are known as "Bed Time Stories", as they are told to children before they sleep. Some times, they are also known as "Fairy Tales", as fairies are usually mentioned in these stories. But, as the children grow, their taste of stories change. They like to hear stories of fights, thrill, horror, etc. The Holy Bible contains stories of all types to suit the taste of children of all ages and even adults. It is for the mothers to choose stories of different types to suit the taste of children of all ages.

Story telling is an art by itself. The mothers, as well as the Sunday School teachers should learn the technique of telling a story to make it very interesting to children of all ages. Telling a story with the help of relevant pictures is more effective in fixing up the story in the minds of little, children particularly. This is exactly the reason, why the children should be shown biblical pictures, as they will be able to remember the Bible story forever by watching a film.

For the guidance and quick reference of all mothers, the entire contents of the Old Testament, New Testament, in brief, all the stories, parables, miracles in Old Testament and New Testament and some special subjects have been explained in the following chapters, as mentioned under the Sunday Schools earlier.

4.

Contents of Each Book of the Old Testament and New Testament of the Holy Bible, in Brief

The Holy Bible is the most precious and widely read book in the entire world. Nearly 2000 years ago, our Lord and Saviour Jesus Christ said, "Heaven and earth will disappear, but my words will remain forever. (Mark 13:31 and Luke 21:33). These precious words of our Lord are true till today and will forever more.

The Holy Bible says (II Timothy 3:16 and 17), "All scriptures is God-breathed and is useful for teaching, rebuking, correcting and training in righteousness, so that the man of God may be thoroughly equipped for every good work."

Here, all scripture means, every word in the Old Testament and New Testament are God breathed. This means, these words are inspired by God, through selected authors of each book in both the Testaments. This gift of God in the shape of the Holy Bible enables us to think of God every moment and maintain intimate relationship with God and seek His guidance and help in whatever we do, day after day.

In the present days, many Presidents of different countries, Kings, High Dignatories, Evangelists and even the people of other faiths in the entire world have accepted the Holy Bible as the "Precious Gift of God to humanity and it is the voice of the Holy Spirit."

As mentioned earlier in this book, there are 39 books in the Old Testament and 27 books in the New Testament. Thus, a total of 66 books in the Holy Bible. The different books in the Holy Bible had been written originally in three languages – Hebrew, Greek and Aramaic during the years 1500 B.C. to 100 A.D. Aramaic language (Different from Arabic language) was the language spoken by Jesus and his disciples. Some scholars say that all the books of the Old Testament were written in Hebrew language with the exception of a few chapters in Ezra, Jeremiah and Daniel. These were written in Aramaic language. All the books of the New Testament were written in Greek language, which was widely spoken in Jesus' time. During the last few years, many scholars were engaged in the Holy Land to translate all the books of the Old Testament and New Testament from different languages into English. Even now, many scholars are working on translation of the entire Holy Bible into different languages spoken in different countries. In India, the Bible Society of India, Bangalore is carrying out the translation of the Holy Bible into different languages spoken in different states of India.

In the beginning, in the year 383 A.D. St. Jerome (Heranius) went at the request of Pope, St.Damasus of Rome to Bethlehem and stayed there for a number of years to translate the entire Holy Bible into Latin language, spoken widely in the Holy Land at that time. This Latin Bible was used for about 1000 years by the Roman Catholic Christians, as they knew Latin language very well. But, as Latin language was not known to many Christians and English language was very well known, during the years 1320 to 1384 A.D., an English scholar by name, John Wycliffe translated the entire Holy Bible into English language. The English version of the Holy Bible appeared in the year

1380 A.D. In the year 1604 A.D., King James I of England appointed a committee of 50 scholars to revise the entire English version of the Holy Bible. King James version of English Bible came out in the year 1611 A.D.

Though all Christians are quite conversant with the entire contents of the Holy Bible, for quick reference to find out any particular story or event in the Bible by the Sunday School teachers and the members of the Women's Fellowship or any other Christians, the contents of each book of the Old Testament and New Testament have been brought out briefly, as mentioned earlier in this book.

4-A: CONTENTS OF THE THIRTY-NINE BOOKS OF THE OLD TESTAMENT, IN BRIEF

All the 39 books of the Old Testament can be grouped into the following four parts:-

PART I: The Pentateuch, or the five books of Moses. The term "Pentateuch" in Greek means, five volumed. These first five books of the Old Testament are also known as "Torah" by the Jews and it is their Bible and they read only Torah on Sabbath days. Brief contents of these five books are explained below:-

BOOK NO.: 1 – GENESIS

This book was written by Moses.

The word "Genesis" means, generation of the universe consisting of heaven and earth with its inhabitants of human beings (Adam and Eve), trees, fowls of the air, beasts, water creatures, etc. Genesis describes the sin committed by Adam and Eve and how God was angry with them and sent them away from the Garden of Eden. The lives of Cain and Abel, the two sons of Adam and Eve, Noah and the flood, Abraham, his son Issac, Jacob, Esau and the interesting story of Joseph in Egypt are explained. In the present days, people believe that the Garden of Eden, where Adam and Eve were placed by God was in the country of Iraq. The remaining events of this book happened in Egypt and Canaan (now known as Israel).

BOOK NO.: 2 – EXODUS

This book was written by Moses.

The word "Exodus" means, departure (of the Israelites from Egypt). This book explains all the difficulties experienced by Israelites as slaves under King Pharaoh of Egypt. Birth of Moses, his adoption by the princess of Egypt, and when she saw him floating in river Nile are explained. Moses's attempts to liberate the Israelites from the hands of Pharoah and lead them to Canaan, the Promised Land of God, infliction of the ten plauges by God on Egyptians, at last the Israelites crossing the Red Sea under the guidance of Moses are explained. Moses met Lord Jehovah on Mount Sinai and heard the Lord speaking to him from the thick cloud on the mountain. Lord Jehovah gave Moses the ten Commandments on two tablets of stone, on Mount Sinai.

The most important point to be noted here is that according to Exodus 32:16, the tablets were the work of God, and the writing was the writing of God, engraved upon the tablets. Verse 15 says that the tablets were written on both sides; written on the front and on the back. Exodus 31:18 says that the two tablets of stone were written with the finger of God.

Exodus 20:1to17, describe the ten Commandments, which every child should learn by heart and remember forever. The ten Commandments, in simple language are as follows:-

1. I am the Lord thy God, and you shall have no other God, except me.

2. Thou shalt not worship any image.

3. Thou shalt not take the name of the Lord lightly and in vain.

4. Thou shalt keep the Sabbath Day, as Holy.

5. Thou shalt honour thy father and mother, so that your days on the land may be long.

6. Thou shalt not kill.

7. Thou shalt not commit adultery.

8. Thou shalt not steal.,

9. Thou shalt not bear false witness against thy neighbour, and

10. Thou shalt not covet anything of your neighbour.

According to Exodus 32:15 to 28, when Moses and Joshua came down the Mount Sinai with two tablets of ten Commandments in the hands of Moses, they heard a noise of people in the camp and they saw that the people were worshipping a golden calf, dancing before it. Moses was very much annoyed to see this and in anger, he threw the two tablets of ten Commandments and broke them to pieces. Moses burnt the golden calf and mixed its ash with water and made the Israelites drink it. As ordered by God, the Levites killed three thousand men on that day for the sin they committed.

According to Exodus 34:1 to 6, the Lord asked Moses to get two tablets of stone like the earlier stones broken by Moses and bring up to Mount Sinai and he would write the words that were in the first tablets. Moses hewed two tablets and went up to Mount Sinai and was there for forty days and forty nights without eating bread or drinking water. Moses came down the mountain along with Aaron and Moses' face was shining as he had seen God. He called all the Israelites and explained the ten Commandments of God.

According to Exodus 31:12 to 17, and 34:21 and 35:2 and 3, the Lord explained to Moses on Mount Sinai how the Israelites should observe the seventh day, as Sabbath day.

According to Exodus, full chapters of 25 to 31, the Lord explained all the details as to how the Israelites should make the Ark of the Covenant, the Tabernacle, Altar and all other items of worship.

When Moses and Aaron came down from Mount Sinai, Moses explained to all Israelites all about Sabbath and making of the Ark as explained to him by the Lord on Mount Sinai.

Details of Ark of the Covenant, the ten Commandments and observance of Sabbath are explained as separate chapters in this book.

BOOK NO.: 3 – LEVITICUS

Moses wrote this book.

This book explains all about the priests of Leviticus, who belong to the tribe of Levi. This book deals mostly with the different laws, purity of priests and their offerings. The five Annual Festivals of Israelites like, i) Feast of Passover, ii) Feast of Pentecost, iii) Feast of Trumpets, iv) The Day of Atonement, v) Feast of Tabernacles are explained in this book. God explains to people as to how to worship him and live holy lives.

BOOK NO.: 4 – NUMBERS

This book was written by Moses.

This book deals with the numbering of the new generations of Israelites, as the older generations passed away during the long journey from Egypt. The book also deals with legislations, Israelites leaving Mount Sinai towards the Promised Land of Canaan, appointment of seventy elders, forty years of journey of Israelites in the wilderness of Sinai, the murmurings of Israelites against Moses and God for not having good food and drinking water and God sending fiery serpents, Moses erecting a Brass Serpent on Mount Nebo to save Israelites bitten by fiery serpents, as ordered by God and finally Moses climbing up to mount Nebo to only see the promised Land of Canaan as said by God and the death of Moses are explained in this book. God was angry with Moses, as Moses did not obey God's words at "Meribah" where water was struck out of a stone. According to Numbers 20:7 to 13 when the Israelites came to the desert of Zin in the first month and they abode in Kadesh and Miriam died there, there was no water and they murmured against Moses and God and Moses and Aaron went to the tabernacle and fell on their faces. The Lord spoke to Moses, saying "Take the rod and gather all Israelites together and speak to the rock before your eyes and it shall give forth water for all Israelites and their beasts, to drink."

Moses did all as commanded by God, but he smote the rock twice with his rod instead of just speaking to the rock as commanded by God. So, the Lord was annoyed at Moses and said, "Because ye believed me not, to sanctify me in the eyes of the children of Israel, therefore, ye shall not bring this congregation into the land, which I have given them. According to the words of God; Moses could not enter Canaan, the Promised Land, but died on Mount Nebo.

BOOK NO.: 5 – DEUTERONOMY

This book was also written by Moses.

The term "Deuteronomy" means, Second Law. The first law was made for the Israelites who lived in Egypt and those who travelled up to Mount Sinai by travelling for forty years through wilderness and deserts and many of them died during this long period. So, a new law called Second Law was necessary as the new generations were entering the Promised Land of Canaan. This book is full of Moses' advice to the Israelites to obey God's commandments, how they should observe the laws in the new Promised Land of Canaan and the final blessings of Moses on all the Israelites. Finally, Moses simply saw the Promised Land of Canaan from Mount Nebo but could not enter it as commanded by God. Moses died on Mount Nebo and was buried in the nearby valley, and no one knows his burial place till now.

PART II : This part contains twelve Historical books from the book of Joshua to the book of Esther, which deal with the history of Israel.

BOOK NO.: 6 – JOSHUA

This book was written by Joshua, who succeeded Moses in leading the Israelites into the Promised Land of Canaan (now known as Israel). The entry of Israelites into Canaan by crossing the big river Jordan, near Jericho is very interesting.

God spoke to Joshua and asked him to be strong and of a good courage as God will be with him always and will not fail him or forsake him.

According to Joshua 3:1 to 17, Joshua ordered the priests, the Levites to carry the Ark of the Covenant ahead of all the Israelites and as soon as the feet of the priests dipped in the brim of the water in river Jordan, the waters which came down from above stopped and the priests stood firm on dry ground in the midst of river Jordan and all the Israelites crossed river Jordan on dry ground, and they were about forty thousand in number. As a sign of crossing the river Jordan on dry land, God told Joshua that the twelve tribes of Israelites should pick up twelve stones from the river bed and place them at the point where the feet of the priests touched the river water, near Gilgal.

After crossing of river Jordan, all the Israelites came to the plains of Jericho. As commanded by Lord, Joshua made seven priests bearing seven trumpets of ram's horns passed on before the Lord and blew with the trumpets: and the Ark of the covenant of the Lord followed them. The priests blew the trumpets and armed men went before them and rear guard came after the Ark of the Lord. For six days, every day they all went round the city of Jericho once and returned to the camp. On the seventh day, as commanded by Joshua they went round the city of Jericho seven times and at the seventh time, when the priests blew the trumpets, Joshua said to the people to shout and when they all shouted, the wall of the city of Jericho fell and the Israelites destroyed the city, killing everyone, except the family members of Rahab, who earlier saved the two spies of Israelites. When the Israelites came to Gibeon, Joshua made peace with them. Five Kings of Amorites - Kings of Jerusalem, Hebron, Jarmuth and Lachish and Eglon joined together and attacked Gibeon. The men of Gibeon sent word to Joshua in Gilgal to come and help them against the five kings. There was a fierce fighting, when Joshua came with Israelites. Joshua ordered the Sun and Moon to stand still till he conquered all the five kings (Chapter 10:13 & 14). At the end of this book of Joshua the farewell address of Joshua and his death are mentioned. The Israelites divided the entire land conquered by them among the 12 tribes.

BOOK NO.: 7 – JUDGES

It is believed that this book was written by Samuel.

This book describes the idolatry of the people and invasions of the Promised Land by enemies from time to time, advises by the thirteen Judges, who delivered the people at times of crisis. God is patient and loves his people, when they obey him. This book also deals with persons like, Deborah, Gideon, Jephthah and mighty Samson (Chapters 4 to 16). God delivered Israelites into the hands of Philistines for forty years.

BOOK NO.: 8 – RUTH

It is believed that this book was written by Samuel, but not clearly known.

This book describes how a simple Moabite woman, Ruth married a Hebrew husband and after his death, started working in the fields of Boaz with her mother-in-law, Naomi. Ruth married Boaz, later on. The book also deals with the birth of a son to Ruth, who became the grandfather of David. Thus, Ruth became an ancestor of Jesus, who belonged to the tribe of David. Ruth and Naomi lived in Bethlehem, which after many years, King David ruled and where after many years Jesus was born.

BOOK NO.: 9 - I SAMUEL

The author of this book is unknown.

This book deals with the birth of Samuel, his prayers to defeat the Philistines, Samuel's prophecy, etc. The book also deals with Saul as the first King of Israel. The story of David and the giant Goliath is described in this book. The fast friendship of David and Jonathan, the son of King Saul, in spite of Saul attempting to kill David by throwing his spear against David and chasing him in caves and mountains are explained. Finally, King Saul's suicide is explained.

BOOK NO.: 10 – II SAMUEL

The author of this book is also unknown.

This book describes the full history of David as a King for forty years. David lamented for the death of King Saul and his son Jonathan, who was David's bosom friend. King David was very anxious to bring the Ark of the Covenant from Baale of Judah to Jerusalem. He chose thirty thousand men and took them to Baale and they placed the Ark on a new cart after bringing it from the house of Abinadab. The two sons of Abinadab, Uzzah and Ahio drove the cart with the Ark on it. As the cart moved, David and all the Israelites, who went with David were playing all kinds of instruments. When they came to Nachon's threshing floor, Uzzah put forth his hand to the Ark of God and took hold of it, as oxen shook it. God was very angry and he smote Uzzah for his error and Uzzah died by the side of the Ark. David was afraid of taking the Ark to the city of David in Jerusalem, but kept it in the house of Obededom the Gittite for three months. This time, the Ark was carried by Levites on shoulders, after David sacrified oxen and fatlings. King David danced as the Ark was reaching the City of David, but his wife Michal, daughter of King Saul, saw King David leaping and dancing before the Ark and she despised him in her heart. The Ark was brought to Jerusalem and placed in the midst of the tabernacle that David had pitched for it and he offered burnt offerings and peace offerings before the Lord. The story of Absalom, the son of King David and his pathetic death as his long hair was caught by an oak tree as he rode on a mule is also described (Chapter 18:8 to 33). King David wept for his son Absalom saying, "O my son Absalom, my son, my son Absolam! Would God I had died for thee, O Absalom, my son, my son"!

King David was keen to build a temple for Jehovah in Jerusalem. The King procured a lot of building materials and cedar wood from Lebanon. But, God did not like King David to construct the temple, as his hands were full of blood due to many battles, he fought.

BOOK NO.: 11 – I KINGS

The author of this book is unknown.

This book deals with the death of King David, who was buried in the City of David in Jerusalem. After David's death, his son Solomon was anointed as the King. King Solomon made friendship with Pharaoh, King of Egypt and married his daughter. One day, King Solomon went to Gibeon to offer sacrifice. When King Solomon was in Gibeon, the Lord appeared to him in a dream and said, "Ask, what I shall give thee." King Solomon thanked the Lord for making him a king of the chosen people of God. So he asked God to give an understanding heart to judge God's people and that he may discern between the good and the bad. This request of King Solomon pleased the Lord and gave to Solomon an understanding heart; so that there was none like him earlier, or in coming years. Though Solomon did not ask God for riches, and honour, God gave these also to Solomon. King Solomon came back to Jerusalem and offered burnt offerings and peace offerings to God in the tabernacle before the Ark of the Covenant.

King Solomon was the king over all Israel. King Solomon's wisdom excelled the wisdom of all people in his country, as well as in Egypt. His fame was in all nations around. King Solomon spoke three thousand proverbs, and one thousand five songs. King Solomon spoke of all trees, all beasts, fowls, and creeping things and of fishes. The Kings from all around the globe came to see King Solomon and to hear him..

Hiram, King of Tyre heard about the fame of King Solomon and sent his people to meet Solomon. King Solomon sent word to King Hiram saying, "You were a friend of my father, King David who desired to build a temple for God. You helped him with cedar wood from Lebanon. But, God did not want my father David to build the temple, as my father's hands were full of blood, as he had fought many battles. God said to my father that his son Solomon should build a house unto my name. So, send to me cedar and fir wood to build the temple. King Hiram was pleased with the words of King Solomon and gave him all help to build the temple in Jerusalem. Thus, King Solomon built a magnificent temple for the Lord in Jerusalem. This is known as the first temple for God. King Solomon invited all elders of Israel to bring the Ark of the Covenant from the city of David on Mount Zion in Jerusalem to the newly built temple of God. The priests brought the Ark and placed it in the temple. The Ark contained the two tablets of stone with Ten Commandments, which Moses placed in the Ark at Mount Horeb. King Solomon dedicated the temple by saying long prayers, and offering burnt offerings and peace offerings. He made big feast to all people.

Queen Sheba heard of the wisdom of King Solomon and visited him, bringing lots of presents of spices, gold, etc. She asked some questions and King Solomon answered them all. She was surprised about the wisdom of King Solomon and his riches also (Chapter 10).

In those days, Prophet Elijah was advising the King now and then. The Prophet said that there would be no rain all these years. God spoke to Elijah and asked him to go and reside by the brook Cherith, that is before river Jordan, drink its water and the ravens will bring bread and flesh in the morning and evening. It was done accordingly. As there was no rain, the brook Cherith dried up and there was no water for Prophet Elijah to drink. God asked Prophet Elijah to leave that place and go to Zarephath and he had commanded a widow there to feed him. As Prophet Elijah reached the gates of city Zarephath, he saw a woman gathering sticks. He asked her to give him bread and water. She said that she had only a small quantity of meal in a barrel and a little oil, which were just sufficient for her and her son. The Lord said that the barrel of meal and oil would not get exhausted till it rained on earth. It happened like that. After some days, the son of that widow fell sick and was breathless. She pleaded to Elijah and he made him live by praying to God (Chapter 17).

Prophet Elijah went to Mount Carmel and told them, "you have kept aside the commandments of the Lord and are following Baal. I am only one as the Prophet of the Lord, but there are four hundred fifty Prophets of your God Baal. Let us prove, which God is the living God. Let them select a bullock and cut it into pieces and place it on wood with no fire under the wood. I will also do with another bullock." The four hundred fifty Prophets of Baal prayed from morning till noon to their God Baal asking him to consume the burnt offering. But, there was no response. Elijah ridiculed them saying that Baal must be sleeping, wake him up by shouting. The four hundred fifty Prophets of Baal shouted more and more but no result. But, Elijah, when his turn came, he built an altar with twelve stones according to the number of tribes, placed the cut pieces of bullock on wood, asked the people to pour four barrels of water on burnt offering and wood. He asked them to do it three times and they did so and the altar was soaked in water. Then, Prophet Elijah prayed to God, when fire of the Lord fell and consumed the burnt offering, as well as the wood, the stones, dust and even the water. When people saw this, they fell on their faces: and said, "The Lord, he is the God: the Lord, he is the God." Elijah asked the people to kill all the four hundred fifty Prophets of Baal and Elijah brought them down to the brook Kishon and slew them there. To commemorate this event, even now there is a huge statue of Prophet Elijah on Mount Carmel with Elijah raising his hand with a sword in his hand and a head of Prophet of Baal under the foot of Elijah (Chapter 18).

The Lord said to Prophet Elijah to go to the wilderness of Damascus and anoint two kings and Elisha, the son of Shaphat as a Prophet in his place. Elijah found Elisha ploughing with twelve yoke of oxen and Elijah passed by him, and cast his mantle upon him. Elisha left the oxen and asked Elijah to permit him to go and kiss his father and mother and Elijah allowed him to do so. Elisha came back and followed Prophet Elijah (Chapter 19:15 to 21).

BOOK NO.: 12 – II KINGS

The author of this book is also unknown.

This book deals mainly with the two Prophets, Elijah and Elisha.

King Ahaziah fell down from the upper chamber in Samaria and was sick. He sent messengers to enquire of Baal Baal-zebub the God of Ekron, whether he would recover.

The Lord said to Elijah to meet the messengers of the king and tell them that because there is no God of Israel that you are enquiring from Baalzebub the God of Ekron. Your king will not recover but die and Elijah departed. The king realized that it was Elijah who said to his messengers like this. So, the King sent his captains twice along with fifty people. But Elijah made fire come down from heaven and consume them all. The third captain with fifty men were saved by Elijah, as they accepted the Lord. The King died as prophesized by Elijah.

Elijah accompanied by Elisha went from Gilgal to Bethel. From there, they went to Jericho and then to Jordan. Fifty men of the sons of the Prophets also were watching as Elijah and Elisha went to river Jordan. Elijah took his mantle, and wrapped it together, and smote the water in river Jordan, when the water got separated and both of them crossed the river on dry bed. Then Elijah said to Elisha, "Ask what I shall do for you, before I be taken away from you." Elisha asked for a double portion of Elijah's spirit on him. Elijah said, "You asked for a hard thing nevertheless, if you see me when I am taken away from you it shall be so to you: but if not, it shall not be so."

As both of them were talking and going, a chariot of fire, and horses of fire parted them and Elijah went up by a whirlwind into heaven. When Elisha saw this, he cried saying, "My father, my father" and he saw him no more. Elisha tore his clothes into two pieces. Elisha took the mantle of Elijah that fell from him and smote the water of river Jordan when the water got separated and Elisha crossed on dry land.

When Elisha was in Jericho, the people came to him and said that the water was naught and the ground was barren in Jericho. Elisha asked them to bring salt and he went to the spring of the waters and cast the salt in it and the water was fit for drinking and irrigation of fields. This spring known as "Elisha spring" still exists in Jericho.

Elisha went from Jericho to Bethel, when children came out of the city, and said, "Go up thou, bald head!; go up thou bald head"! Elisha cursed them and two female bears came out of the woods and killed forty two of the children. Then, Elisha went to Carmel and from there to Samaria (Chapter 2).

Elisha performed many miracles – A widow had two sons and her creditors were taking the two sons as bondmen. She went to Prophet Elisha and requested him to help her. Elisha asked her to tell what all she had in the house. She said she only had a pot of oil. Elisha asked her to go to her neighbours and borrow as many empty vessels as possible and pour the oil into each vessel little by little. All the vessels were filled with oil. She sold the oil and paid the debt and lived peacefully (Chapter 4:1 to 7).

Whenever Elisha was passing through Shunem, he was eating bread with one woman. She constructed a room for Elisha. One day, Elisha called her and asked her what she wanted. She said nothing. Elisha came to know that she had no children and told her, that at a particular season, she will have a son. Accordingly, she gave birth to a boy. One day, the boy fell seriously ill, and died. She hurriedly took the boy on an ass to Mount Carmel as Elisha was staying there. Elisha made this boy live and handed him over to his mother (Chapter 4: 8 to 37).

Elisha came to Gilgal, where there was acute shortage of food. One person went into the fields and brought wild gourds, cooked them, and served to the people. While eating, they cried out that there was death in the pot. Elisha threw a meal into the pot and they all ate with no harm (Chapter 4:38 to 41).

Elisha fed one hundred people with only twenty loaves of barley and full ears of corn and still much food was left thereof, (Chapter 4:42 to 44).

Naaman was a captain in the army of Syria. He was a leper. He had a little maid servant from Israel. One day, she told him of Elisha in Israel to cure him. Naaman came in a chariot to the door of Elisha. Elisha sent a messenger to Naaman, saying, "Go, and wash in river Jordan seven times and be cured." Naaman was angry, as Elisha did not even come out to meet him and said, "Are there no rivers like Abana and Pharpar in Damascus, which have better waters than river Jordan in Israel?" Naaman went away in anger. His servants persuaded Naaman to do as said by Elisha. Naaman went to river Jordan and dipped himself seven times in the Jordan water, when his flesh became like that of a child. Naaman came to Elisha to thank him and offer rich gifts, but Elisha did not accept the gifts. Naaman went away. But the servant of Elisha followed Naaman and got a few gifts from Naaman, and returned. Elisha came to know about this and punished his servant by giving him the leprosy of Naaman and the servant went out as a leper, as white as snow (Chapter 5).

The sons of the Prophets said to Elisha that they should make a dwelling near Jordan river. When they came to Jordan, they started cutting wood. As one of them was felling a beam, the axe head fell into the water. The person cried, as it was a borrowed axe. He came to Elisha and told him of it. Elisha asked him where it fell, and Elisha cut down a stick and cast it at the exact place, when the axe floated up and the man took it, joyfully (Chapter 6:1 to 7).

Prophet Elisha performed many such miracles and prophesied also about the future of different kings.

BOOK NO.: 13 – I CHRONICLES

The author of this book is unknown, but believed to have been edited by Ezra.

Chapters 1 to 9, deals with the names of different generations of Israelites.

From Chapters 10 to 29, it is more or less repetition of what is written in I and II Samuel, mentioned earlier in this book. These chapters deal with the death of King Saul, and David succeeding Saul as the King. King David brought the Ark of the Covenant to Jerusalem with all people singing and dancing before the Ark. David himself, though a king, danced before the Ark. His wife, Michal saw him through the window and she despised him in heart. King David had a great desire to build a temple for Jehovah in Jerusalem. He procured expensive cedar wood and many precious articles for the temple. But, the Lord did not like David to construct the temple, as David's hands were full of blood, due to many battles he fought. God wanted that King David's son, King Solomon to build a temple. David died, and his son Solomon was made the King (For more details of the Ark of the Covenant and tabernacle etc, see the separate chapter at the end of this book).

BOOK NO.: 14 – II CHRONICLES

Some scholars say that Ezra wrote this Book.

A few portions in this book are repetition of what is written in the Books of I and II Samuel, mentioned earlier in this book.

King Solomon successfully constructed a magnificent temple for the Lord Jehovah in Jerusalem on Mount Moriah, where the Lord appeared to King David, his father.

King Solomon sent a word to King Hiram of Tyre, saying that he should be kind to him as he was to his father King David and send Cedar, Fir and Algum wood from Lebanon and also skilled workers to work on gold, silver, brass and iron to make for the temple (Chapter 2:1 to 10).

In chapters 3,4 and 5, King Solomon instructed every detail of the temple. King Solomon assembled all priests and people to bring the Ark of the Covenant from the city of David on Mount Zion to the temple. There was nothing in the Ark, except the two tablets of stone with the Ten Commandments, which Moses put in on Mount Horeb (Chapter 5:1 to 10). Solomon called all people at the temple for its dedication. King Solomon made very long prayers (Chapter 6). When King Solomon had made an end of praying, the fire came down from heaven and consumed the burnt offering. The Lord appeared to Solomon by night, and said unto him, that if he walked before him, as David, his father and observe all God's statues, he would bless him abundantly (Chapter 7).

Chapter 9 deals with the visit of Queen of Sheba bringing lots of precious gifts and feeling satisfied that King Solomon was really wise and was a rich King. This is repetition of a portion already mentioned under I Kings (Chapter 9:1 to 12).

Chapters 10 to 35 deal with different kings, one after the other. King Solomon ruled for forty years and died and was buried in the city of David.

When Jehoiakim was the King of Judah and Jerusalem, Nebuchadnezzar, King of Babylon raided Jerusalem and carried away King Jehoiakim with fetters to Babylon. Nebuchadnezzar looted the temple also and carried all expensive vessels etc., to Babylon and placed them in his temple in Babylon. King of Chaldees raided Jerusalem and killed every one, young and old, burnt the house of God, broke the walls of Jerusalem and burnt all places and took many people as slaves to Babylon (Chapter 36:1 to 21). Chapter 36:22 to 23 say that in the first year of Cyrus, King of Persia, the Lord stirred up the spirit of Cyrus to make a proclamation in his kingdom, saying that the Lord charged him to build his house in Jerusalem and invited all people to join him in this activity.

BOOK NO.: 15 – EZRA

The author of the book is unknown, but some scholars believe that it was written by Ezra.

King Cyrus collected many precious gifts of gold, silver and even the vessels of the house of the Lord which King Nebuchadnezzar brought from Jerusalem and placed in the house of his Gods and took them all to Jerusalem. Chapter 2 deals with the names of all Israelites who were carried away to Babylon as slaves by King Nebuchadnezzar and now returned to their places in Jerusalem. They were about forty thousand three hundred seventy two and their maids, cattle, etc.

All of them started constructing the temple. After King Cyrus, King Darius ruled. In the sixth year of King Darius regime, the temple was completed. All the children of Israel dedicated it with great joy.

Then, Ezra was the chief priest. Chapter 10 deals with the Israelites taking strange women of Babylon as their wives and some had children with these women. This is a great transgression. Ezra appointed two judges to judge these men until the fierce wrath of the Lord for this matter is turned from them.

BOOK NO.: 16 – NEHEMIAH

The author of this book is unknown, but some scholars believe that it was written by Ezra.

Nehemiah was server of wine in a cup to the King of Persia. He heard from one person, who came from Judah that the walls of Jerusalem had been destroyed and gates burnt. Nehemiah was sad and while serving wine, the king asked him why he was sad. Nehemiah requested him to send him to Judah so that he could reconstruct the walls and gates of Jerusalem. The king gave him letters to help him with wood and other building materials and a few people to help Nehemiah. After many days, Nehemiah could rebuild the broken gates and walls of Jerusalem with the help of many Jews in Jerusalem. Nehemiah saw the register of genealogy of all those who returned from Babylon to Jerusalem. Ezra, the priest brought the book of Law of Moses and read it to all Israelites. They were all happy and vowed to go by the Law of Moses. After all this work of rebuilding the walls and gates of Jerusalem, Nehemiah went back from Jerusalem, to Persia.

BOOK NO.: 17 – ESTHER

The author of this book is unknown.

This book deals with the beautiful story of Esther, a Jew girl who saved all Jews in Persia.

One day, the King of Persia made a big dinner to all princes and many people. When the dinner was on, the king called his wife by name, Vashti to appear before all the assembled princes. The queen refused to appear. The king of Persia was very angry with the queen for refusing his orders, and he dethroned her. Then, the king was in search of a beautiful girl as his wife and to be the queen of Persia.

There was a Jew by the name, Mordecai working in the palace of the king. He had an adopted daughter by the name, Esther. She was very beautiful. So, Mordecai showed her to the king. The king liked Esther and married her and made her the queen of Persia. Once, a court official planned to kill the king. Mordecai knew about the plot and told it to the king and thus, saved his life.

There was a man by the name Haman in the palace. The king promoted him to a high position. But, Mordecai did not respect Haman. So, Haman plotted to kill all the Jews residing in Persia. He got gallows erected to hang Mordecai. Mordecai knew this plot and told Esther about this plot. Esther wept before the king and told him about this plot to kill all the Jews. The king was angry and asked his soldiers to hang Haman on the gallows prepared by him to hang Mordecai. The king made Mordecai as the Prime Minister of Persia. Thus, Esther saved all the Jews residing in Persia. The book of Esther shows how God takes care of his people, as he has power over all kings and rulers.

PART– III: POETICAL BOOKS: The next five books in the Holy Bible are known as poetical books. These are the books of Job, Psalms, Proverbs, Ecclesiastes, and Song of Solomon. The authors of these books used poetry to express many feelings from sadness to happiness, from fear to praise to God for his protection and love.

BOOK NO.: 18 – JOB

The author of this book is unknown.

This book deals with the life of Job, who was a perfect and an upright man, and who, feared God. Job had seven sons and three daughters. They were happy as Job had many cattle, servants and all riches. They were meeting in each brother's house in turns for dinners. One day, when they were all eating and drinking in eldest brother's house, the servants came and told Job that his oxen, asses, sheep's, servants were killed. Due to a great wind, the house in which his seven sons and three daughters were dining collapsed and many died. Job rent his clothes, shaved and fell on the ground. He said, "Naked came I out of my mother's womb, and naked shall I return thither: The Lord gave, and the Lord hath taken away, blessed be the name of the Lord." But satan was against Job. He smote Job with sore boils throughout his body. Job's wife asked Job to curse God, and die. But, Job said to her not to talk foolishly, as they received many good things from God and they should receive evil also. Three friends of Job came to Job to comfort him.

Chapters 3 to 37 deals with the ill advice of the three friends of Job.

But, the Lord answered Job out of the whirlwind comforting him for his righteousness. The Lord spoke to the three friends of Job, as they did not speak of him the thing that is right, as Job spoke. So, God asked them to offer burnt offerings and go to Job, who would pray for them. God blessed Job by giving him twice as much as he had earlier. All the relatives and friends of Job did eat bread with Job. Lord blessed Job at the end more than at the beginning. Job distributed all his property to his seven sons and three daughters and saw his four generations, and died at an old age.

BOOK NO.: 19 – PSALMS

The scholars believe that out of all the one hundred fifty Psalms, as many as seventy three were written by King David and hence, these Psalms are usually known as Psalms of David. The remaining seventy seven Psalms are believed to have been written by the sons of Korah, Asaph, Solomon, Moses, Ezra, etc.

All the Psalms are spiritual songs read or sung in the church services and devotional meetings. Different Psalms depict different topics, like how to thank God, how to love God, religious experiences, etc. Usually, Sunday School children and other school children are asked to learn by heart, some popular Psalms such as Psalm 23 – "The Lord is my shepherd etc., etc.", Psalm 121 – "I will lift up mine eyes unto the hills, from whence cometh my help etc., etc", and a few more.

BOOK NO.: 20 – PROVERBS

The author of this book is not very well known, but may be King Solomon.

As mentioned earlier in this book under the heading of I Kings, three thousand Proverbs and one thousand five Songs were written by King Solomon.

These proverbs are more or less advices for a good living, contrast between good and bad, qualities of good and bad women, ideal wife, etc.

BOOK NO.: 21 – ECCLESIASTES

The exact author of this book is not known, but may be King Solomon, as many instances mentioned in this book are the experiences of King Solomon. The exact meaning of the term "Ecclesiastes" is "Preacher." This book explains the monotonous life of a man and his search for happiness, which cannot be achieved by wealth, wisdom, art, etc. But, the conclusion is "Fear God, and keep his commandments for this is the whole duty of a man. For God shall bring every work into judgement, with every secret thing, whether it be good, or whether it be evil" (Chapter 12:13,14).

BOOK NO.: 22 – SONG OF SOLOMON

As it name itself indicates, the author of this book is King Solomon. As mentioned earlier in this book under the heading of I Kings, three thousand proverbs and one thousand five songs were written by King Solomon.

This book is a beautiful poem. It tells about the love between a man and a woman. This book also shows us God's love for his people.

PART – IV: PROPHETICAL BOOKS

The next seventeen books are known as prophetical books, as they deal with five major prophets – Isaiah, Jeremiah, Ezekiel, Daniel, Lamentations and twelve minor Prophets like, Hosea, Joel, Amos, Obadiah, Jonah, Micah, Nahum, Habakkuk, Zephaniah, Haggai, Zechariah and Malachi.

MAJOR PROPHETS

BOOK NO.: 23 – ISAIAH

It is believed that Prophet Isaiah wrote this book.

Prophet Isaiah is considered to be the greatest of the Prophets of the Old Testament.

Chapter 9:6 says, "For unto us a child is born, unto us a son is given; and the government shall be upon his shoulder: and his name shall be called wonderful, Counsellor, The Mighty God, the Everlasting Father, The Prince of Peace." Thus, Prophet Isaiah prophesied about the coming of Messiah. Prophet Isaiah warned the people about the judgement of Messiah. He prophesized about the surrounding nations and salvation. King Hezekiah of Judah was attacked by the King of Assyria, but Prophet Isaiah said the King of Assyria would go back defeated and fall by his sword in his country. It happened like that when King Hezekiah was sick, Prophet Isaiah met him and said that he would die. Hezekiah turned his face towards the wall, and prayed, saying, how he walked before the Lord in truth and perfect heart, and wept bitterly. God pitied him and sent Prophet Isaiah to tell Hezekiah that his life would be extended by fifteen years (Chapter 38: 1 to 5).

Chapter 53: 3 to 7 says, "He is despised and rejected of men. He hath borne our griefs and carried our sorrows. He was wounded for our transgressions, he was bruised for our iniquities and with his stripes we are healed. We all have gone astray like sheep. He was oppressed and he was afflicted, yet he opened not his mouth: he is brought as lamb to the slaughter and as a sheep before her shearers is dumb, so he openeth not his mouth."

In Chapter 65: 17 to 25, the Lord said, "Behold, I create new heaven and a new earth: and the former shall not be remembered, not come into mind. I create Jerusalem a rejoicing and her people a joy. I will rejoice in Jerusalem, weeping shall no more be heard in Jerusalem. The wolf and the lamb shall feed together, and the lion shall eat straw like the bullock; and dust shall be serpent's meat. They shall not hurt nor destroy in all my holy mountain."

BOOK NO.: 24 – JEREMIAH

This book was written by Prophet Jeremiah himself during the time when the kingdom was split into Israel and Judah.

The Lord told Jeremiah (Chapter 1: 4 to 9), before I formed thee in the belly, I knew thee; and before thou camest forth out of the womb I sanctified thee, and ordained thee as a Prophet unto the nations." When Jeremiah said that he was a child and could not speak, the Lord said, "Be not afraid of any one, for I am with thee to deliver thee." The Lord put forth his hand, and touched Jeremiah's mouth and said, " Behold, I have put my words in thy mouth, and I have set thee over all nations, and the people will fight against thee but they shall not prevail against thee, for I am with thee, to deliver thee." The Lord said to Jeremiah (Chapter 2:2), "Go and cry in the ears of Jerusalem that they have forsaken me and my fear is not in thee."

Chapter 5 onwards God told Prophet Jeremiah, how Israelites had disobeyed his statues and unless they amend their ways and doings, they will not be able to reside in the Land of Canaan given to their fathers by God. God's anger and fury shall be poured upon them and it shall burn everything. God warned the people against idolatry, as the idols are a molten image with no breath in them (Chapter 10:14). In Chapter 17:20 to 27, God asked Jeremiah to tell all people in Judah and Jerusalem, to observe Sabbath in the way commanded by their fathers and do no work, otherwise, God will kindle a fire, which will devour the palaces of Jerusalem. In Chapter 23, God warned all the people about false prophets, who ill-advised all people and made them forget God's name telling that they dreamt of their advice. God will surely punish them all suitably.

In Chapter 27, Jeremiah foretold about King Nebuchadnezzar of Babylon taking away everything from Jerusalem. In Chapter 28:2 to 3, God said that within two full years, he would bring again to Jerusalem, all the vessels of the Lord's house Nebuchadnezzar carried to Babylon. In Chapter 30:3 it is said that the Lord will bring again the people of Israel and Judah from captivity in Babylon. Chapter 31 shows that God's love lasts forever.

Chapter 32:1 to 4 says that, when Zedekiah was the king of Judah, Nebuchadnezzar, the king of Babylon besieged Jerusalem and Jeremiah was shut up in the court of the prison, which was in the king of Judah's house. The Lord, the God of Israel asked Jeremiah to go and tell Zedekiah, king of Judah that God will give this city into the hands of the King of Babylon, and he shall burn it with fire and Zedekiah will be taken to Babylon (Chapter 34:2 to 5). Chapter 39:1 to 12 says that the King of Babylon and all his army attacked King Zedekiah and besieged Jerusalem. King Zedekiah fled by night into the plains. But, the Chaldeans army pursued after him and caught him in the plains of Jericho. They brought King Zedekiah and his sons to King Nebuchadnezzar, when he killed all the sons and nobles of Zedekiah. He put out King Zedekiah's eyes and bound him in chains to carry him to Babylon. The army burnt all palaces, gates and walls of Jerusalem. Prophet Jeremiah was allowed to stay in Judah, itself.

BOOK NO.: 25 – LAMENTATIONS

This book is believed to have been written by Prophet Jeremiah himself, after Jerusalem was destroyed and many Israelites were carried away by the King Nebuchadnezzar as slaves in Babylon. This book is also known as the "Lamentations of Jeremiah." Lamentations means, Songs of Sadness.

Lord Jehovah, who was protecting Israel all these days, forsook its inhabitants, the Israelites due to their sins, idolatry and forgetting to follow the statutes of the Lord. King

Nebuchadnezzar attacked Judah and Jerusalem and destroyed everything there and took many Israelites as slaves to his country, Babylon. Jerusalem was desolate. Jeremiah, who was left behind was very much troubled about the sufferings of Israelites as slaves in Babylon and his own sufferings. Prophet Jeremiah prayed to God for his mercy. Israelites realized their sins and repented and pleaded with God to renew their days, as of old.

BOOK NO.: 26 – EZEKIEL

This book was written by Prophet Ezekiel, who was a prisoner in Babylon.

Ezekiel was a priest in the Land of Chaldeans by the river Chebar in Babylon. When he was standing by the side of river Chebar in Babylon, he saw a vision of a whirlwind, in which he saw four living creatures looking like man with wings. He also saw a throne with a man sitting on it with brightness around him. It was the Lord. Ezekiel fell on his face when he saw the Lord. The Lord said to Ezekiel, "Son of Man, I send thee to the children of Israel, to a rebellious nation that hath rebelled against me and tell them of their sins. You warn the righteous man and if he does not sin, he shall live." The Lord took Ezekiel to many places to see for himself the different types of sins being committed by his people.

God told Ezekiel to go and tell all the mountains, hills, rivers and valleys of Israel that the Lord will bring a sword upon them and will destroy all high places.

In Chapter 20:13 to 24, the Lord said to Ezekiel, that the people of Israel polluted the Sabbaths and hence, he would pour out his fury upon them, and their eyes were after their father's idols.

Chapter 37:1 to 14, Ezekiel had a vision of dry bones in a valley coming together to life.

BOOK NO.: 27 – DANIEL

This book was written by Daniel, the Prophet. This book contains many interesting stories.

When Jehoiakim was the king of Judah, King Nebuchadnezzar, the king of Babylon besieged Jerusalem and carried him as captive to Babylon. Nebuchadnezzar plundered the Jerusalem temple and took away gold and silver cups and many other valuables things to Babylon. The king brought with him many children of Judah as prisoners and as slaves. Among them, Daniel, Shadrach, Meshach and Abednego were also there. Daniel loved God very much and always wanted to live according to God's statues. The king asked his commander to train some people as knowledgeable people to stand before the king and among them Daniel, Shadrach, Meshach and Abednego were also selected. The king ordered that all of them should be given special king's food and wine for three years. But, these four people asked for only pulses to eat, for ten days only and see their health. After ten days of feeding only on pulses, the four were found to be healthier than all those who were fed with the king's food. Daniel had the capacity of understanding of all visions and dreams, whereas the other three were very knowledgeable and skilled. The king found that these four were ten times better than the magicians and astrologers of his kingdom.

One day, King Nebuchadnezzar had a dream and his sleep was broken and his spirit was troubled. He wanted that the dream should be interpreted. All the astrologers and magicians of his country were called to interpret the dream of the king. King Nebuchadnezzar told them that if they could not interpret his dream after hearing it, they would be cut to pieces and their houses made dunghills. If they interpreted the dream properly, they would be rewarded abundantly. The king asked them first tell the dream and then interpret. They all said that it was impossible for human beings to do that and only God could tell the dream and its interpretation. The king was furious at this and commanded destruction of all wise men of Babylon. Daniel and his three companions were also to be slain by the king's soldiers. Daniel asked for time, and he consulted his three companions. That night Daniel had a vision about the dream, when God revealed to Daniel the dream. Daniel thanked the Lord and asked the commander to take him to the king. Daniel told the king that only God in heaven knoweth all secrets. Daniel told the King, "O King, you saw in your dream a great image, whose brightness was excellent. The head of this image was of fine gold, his breast and his arms of silver, his belly and thighs of brass, his legs of iron and his feet partly iron and partly clay. The king saw a stone was cut without hands and which smote the image upon his feet, which were partly of iron and partly of clay and broke them into pieces. Then, other parts of brass, silver and gold were broken to pieces and blown away by the wind. The stone that struck the image became a big mountain." Daniel interpreted this dream by saying, " Thou O King, art King of Kings as the God of Heaven hath given you a kingdom, power, strength and glory. So, in that image, you are the head of gold. After you, another kingdom inferior to your kingdom will come and another third kingdom of brass will come as in the image. The fourth kingdom will be strong as iron, which breaks everything, shall it break in pieces and bruise. The feet and toes of partly iron and partly clay in the image shows that your kingdom shall be divided, but there shall be in it the strength of iron and the kingdom will be partly strong and partly broken as iron and clay as the toes of the image. A stone was cut out without hands and it broke every part of the image into pieces shows that God had made known to thee what shall come to pass hereafter and the dream is certain and the interpretation thereof is sure."

King Nebuchadnezzar was extremely pleased with Daniel, fell on his face and worshipped Daniel. The King said to Daniel, "Your God is a God of Gods and a Lord of Kings and revealer of secrets." The king made Daniel ruler over the whole province of Babylon and chief of the Governors over all the wise men of Babylon. Daniel requested the king to set Shadrach, Meshach and Abednego over the affairs of the province of Babylon and Daniel sat in the gate of the king (Entire Chapter: 2).

Chapter 3 deals with the king making a huge image of gold to be worshipped by all in his kingdom.

At the time of dedication of this statue, a proclamation was made saying that at a time when all musical instruments sound, all people including the princes, governors, etc. should fall down and worship the golden image of King Nebuchadnezzar and whoever failed to do so would be thrown on into burning fiery furnace.

The people reported that Shadrach, Meshach and Abednego, whom the king had set over the affairs of Babylon, had not bowed down. The king was furious and ordered that the furnace should be heated to seven times than earlier and he made the soldiers throw these three men into the furnace. King Nebuchadnezzar rose up and went to the furnace and was surprised to see four people in the burning furnace, instead of three people thrown into it and the fourth person was like the Son of God. The king said, "Shadrach, Meshach and Abednego, ye servants of the most high God, come forth." They all observed that not a single hair of them was burnt. The king made a proclamation saying that whosever spoke against the God of Shadrach, Meshach and Abednego will be cut into pieces. The king promoted these men in the Province of Babylon.

Chapter 5 says that King Belshazzar made a great feast. He commanded that the golden and silver vessels, which his father King Nebuchadnezzar had carried from the temple in Jerusalem should be brought and they all drank wine in them. In the same hour, the king saw figures of a man's handwriting on the wall. The king called all the astrologers in his kingdom to read that writing on the wall, but none could read it. Finally, Daniel was brought to read. Daniel said," You have committed sin by drinking wine in the vessels of the Jerusalem temple. The writing on the wall is - "Mene, Mene, Tekel, U-Pharsin." The interpretation is "Mene means, God hath numbered thy kingdom, and finished it - Tekel means, thou art weighed in the balance, and art found wanting - Peres means, Thy kingdom is divided and given to the Medes and Persians." King Belshazzar honoured Daniel and made him the third ruler in the country of Babylon and that night the king died. Then, Darius took over the kingdom of Babylon.

Chapter 6 says that as Daniel was made first above all presidents and princes in Babylon, they all became jealous and wanted to find an occasion to report to the king about Daniel's fault. They made King Darius sign a law saying, that whosoever pray to any God other than thee for thirty days, shall be cast into the den of lions. Daniel knew about this new law. But, he went into his house and his windows being open towards Jerusalem, prayed three times a day thanking God. The people saw this and reported to the king. The king was displeased with himself, as he wanted to save Daniel. But, the people pressed the king not to change the law, once signed by him. They brought Daniel and he was thrown into the lion's den. The king said, "Daniel, thy God whom thou servest continuously will deliver thee." A big stone was brought to seal the mouth of the den and it was sealed with king's signet and signets of his lords. The king went to his palace and did not eat and had a sleepless night. The king rose very early in the morning and went in haste to the den of lions. He cried out in a lamentable voice saying, "Daniel, O Daniel, servant of the living God, is thy God, whom thou servest continually, able to deliver thee from the lions?." To his great surprise Daniel answered from the den of lions, "O King, my God hath sent his angel and hath shut the lions' mouths, that they have not hurt me." The king was very happy to see Daniel alive and asked his soldiers to get Daniel from the den of lions and throw in it all the men who accused Daniel. King Darius made a law in Babylon, saying that all people should tremble and fear before the God of Daniel: for he is the living God, as he delivered Daniel from the power of the lions. Thus, Daniel prospered in the regime of King Darius and earlier King Cyrus in Babylon.

Daniel interpreted many other dreams of the kings and was highly respected in Babylon. The four people Daniel, Shedrach, Meshach and Abednego were the children of God and became very famous in the kingdom of Babylon.

12 MINOR PROPHETS

From here onwards, twelve minor Prophets of the Old Testament are described.

BOOK NO.: 28 – HOSEA

This book was written by Prophet Hosea.

Israelites were not faithful to God and he was very unhappy about this. Hosea still continued to love them. Hosea warned all the Israelites to lead a good life and get the blessings of God.

BOOK NO.: 29 – JOEL

This book was written by the Prophet Joel, a Prophet of Judah, but not very well known.

Prophet Joel wanted that the people of Judah should stop sinning and feel sorry for their sins. He pleaded with the people for repentance and prayed to God to forgive them. Joel saw giant bugs, which attacked all crops on the land. These bugs were like army, which showed that one day God would send an army to punish the people for their sins. God finally said that Judah should dwell forever and Jerusalem from generation to generation.

BOOK NO.: 30 – AMOS

This book was written by Prophet Amos himself.

Amos was neither a Prophet nor a son of a prophet in the beginning. He was a herd man of Tekoa. God sent him to speak to his people. God said that the Israelites have kept away his commandments and despised the law of the Lord. So, he will send fire upon Judah and it shall devour the palaces of Jerusalem. He said that he brought the Israelites from Egypt and led them forty years through the wilderness to possess the Land of Canaan. But, they commanded the Prophets sent by God not to prophesy. Amos saw five visions – Grasshoppers, Fire, Plumbline, Basket of summer fruit and smitten sanctuary. Amaziah, the priest of Bethel sent to Jeroboam, King of Israel, saying that Amos hath conspired against him by saying Jeroboam shall die by the sword and Israel shall surely be led away captive out to their own land. Amaziah asked Prophet Amos to go to the Land of Judah and prophesy there and not in Bethel, as it is the king's chapel and is the king's court.

But Prophet Amos answered to Amaziah, "I was no prophet, neither was I a prophet's son: but I was a herds man, and a gatherer of sycamore fruit. But the Lord took me as I followed the flock, and the Lord said to me, go, prophesy to my people of Israel." So, Prophet Amos cursed Amaziah (Chapter 7: 10 to 17).

Prophet Amos told the rich people to be kind to the poor, as God cares for the poor also.

BOOK NO.: 31 – OBADIAH

This book was written by Prophet Obadiah.

This book is very short.

This book deals with the enimity between Edom and Israel. The Edomites were descendents of Esau, the brother of Jacob, as Jacob had cheated his brother Esau of his birthright. People of the nation Edom were happy, when Jerusalem was destroyed. They took away things from empty Jerusalem, but Prophet Obadiah warned them that God will punish them, as the people of Israel are Abraham's children and children of God.

BOOK NO.: 32 – JONAH

This book was written by Prophet Jonah.

Jonah was called by God to go to the city of Nineveh and cry against it, as its wickedness had come before God. But, Jonah did not want to obey God's commandment and wanted to escape from it. He went to the port of Joppa and got into a ship that was going to Tarshish. But, the Lord sent out a great wind on to the sea and the ship was tossing severely and was about to break into pieces. All the people in the ship were asked to pray to their Gods to protect themselves. But, Jonah was fast asleep in the ship. They all decided to cast lots to find out as to who was responsible for this curse of storm. The lot fell on Jonah. They woke up Jonah and asked him as to what he had done to invite this curse of God. Jonah realized his sin of disobeying the command of God in not going to Nineveh and asked them to throw him into the sea to subside the storm. But, all of them tried their best to bring the ship to the land, instead of throwing Jonah into the sea. But, they could not bring the ship to the land. So, at last they all threw Jonah into the sea to arrest the storm. But, God made a big fish swallow Jonah. Jonah was in the belly of the fish for three days and three nights. Jonah prayed to God from the belly of the fish. God pardoned Jonah and made the fish vomit Jonah on dry land. This way Jonah was saved from the belly of a great fish in the sea.

God asked Jonah, a second time to go to Nineveh and preach. This time, Jonah obeyed God's command and went to the city of Nineveh. Jonah warned the people of Nineveh to repent and obey the commandments of God, otherwise in forty days time, Nineveh will be overthrown. At this, all the people of Nineveh and the King of Nineveh repented, covering themselves with sack clothes and praying to God. So, God pitied them and forgave them by not destroying the city of Nineveh. But, Jonah was furious, as God forgave them. In fury, Jonah went out of the city of Nineveh and sat under the shadow of a booth. But, God made a plant of gourd to grow overnight to give him shade and protect him from the hot sun. Jonah was happy. But, God made the plant dry up in the next night by getting it eaten by a worm. In the daytime God made a hot wind blow and Jonah fainted due to the hot wind. God told Jonah that he was pitying the gourd plant, which he never planted and can He (God) not pity thousands of people of Nineveh, as they repented for their sins and God forgave them?" Thus, God forgives the people when they repent for their sins and obey God's command.

BOOK NO.: 33 – MICAH

The author of this book was Prophet Micah.

The most important portion of this book is chapter 5:2, which is prophecy about the birth of Jesus. It says, "But thou, Bethlehem, Ephratah though thou be little among the thousands of Judah, yet out of thee shall he come forth unto me that is to be ruler in Israel whose goings forth have been from of old, from everlasting."

Prophet Micah condemned sins like idolatry, dishonesty, corruption, etc. and threatened the people of Judah about the forthcoming judgement and coming of Messiah. Micah also said, "God does not retain his anger for ever, because he delighteth in mercy. God will have compassion on us and he will subdue our inequities and thou will cast all your sins into the depth of the seas."

BOOK NO.: 34 – NAHUM

This book was written by Prophet Nahum.

This book deals with the idolatry of the people of Nineveh, the capital of Assyria. When Prophet Jonah preached to them, they all repented, but later on they were indulged in idolatry. They plundered other nations and their riches were like a lion's den full of its prey. Complete ruin of the city of Nineveh was foretold.

BOOK NO.: 35 – HABAKKUK

This book was written by Prophet Habakkuk.

Prophet Habakkuk prays to God that every one is sinful, but no punishment is given to them. But God revealed his plan to punish these sinners. Prophet Habakkuk prays to God saying, "I will rejoice in the Lord, I will joy in the God of my salvation. The Lord is my strength."

BOOK NO.: 36 – ZEPHANIAH

This book was written by Prophet Zephaniah.

This book deals with the cautioning of the people of their sinful life and warns them of the forthcoming judgement by Lord Jehovah. Prophet Zephaniah called the people for repentance. Finally, he foretold about the coming of happy days and God will save Jerusalem.

BOOK NO.: 37 – HAGGAI

This book was written by Prophet Haggai.

This book deals with the rebuilding of the God's temple in Jerusalem. After all the Israelites returned from captivity in Babylon to Jerusalem, in the regime of King Cyrus of Persia, in the year 535 B.C., they started rebuilding the temple as encouraged by King Cyrus. But due to some reasons, the rebuilding work was stopped. In the second year of the regime of King Darius, Prophet Haggai persuaded the people to start rebuilding the temple, instead of concentrating on the beautification of their own house, after they returned from Babylon. They started rebuilding the temple and they successfully completed the temple reconstruction in the fourth year of the regime of King Darius. This temple was inferior in appearance to the earlier temple built by King Solomon. Finally, Prophet Haggai told the people of the blessings of Lord Jehovah for rebuilding the temple in Jerusalem.

BOOK NO.: 38 – ZECHARIAH

This book was written by Prophet Zechariah.

In the second year of the regime of King Darius the word of the Lord came to Zechariah. He observed sinful life of the people and encouraged them to rebuild the temple in Jerusalem. Prophet Zechariah saw eight visions, which are:

1) A man riding on a red horse and stood among the myrtle trees and behind him, there were red horses, 2) Four horns and four carpenters, 3) A man with a measuring line in his hand, 4) Joshua, the high priest standing before the angel of the Lord and satan standing at his right hand to resist him. Joshua was clothed with filthy garments and stood before the angel. God made his garments change, 5) A golden candle stick with a bowl on its top and seven lamps and seven pipes to the seven lamps. There were two olive trees, one on its right side and another on its left side, 6) A flying roll depicting the curse that goeth forth over the face of the whole earth, 7) An ephah and two women, who lifted up the ephah between the earth and the heaven, and 8) Four chariots coming out of the two mountains, which were of brass, the first chariot drawn by red horses, the second chariot by black horses, the third by white horses and the fourth chariot drawn by grisled and bay horses. An angel explained to Prophet Zechariah the meaning of each vision. (Chapters 1 to 6)

The Lord said to Prophet Zechariah (Chapter 8), "I am returning to Zion, and will dwell in the midst of Jerusalem and Jerusalem will be called a city of truth: and the mountain of the Lord of hosts the holy mountain. Old men and women with sticks in their hands will dwell in the streets of Jerusalem, the streets of Jerusalem shall be full of boys and girls playing."

BOOK NO.: 39 – MALACHI

This book was written by Prophet Malachi.

This is the last book in the Old Testament. In this book also, the sinful life of the children of those who returned from Babylon is explained. Many social sins are committed by these people. Finally, the Lord Jehova said, "They had robbed the Lord by not giving the tithes and offerings. So, there is a curse on them. He would send (chapter 4:5) Elijah, the Prophet before the coming of the great and dreadful day of the Lord. Elijah will turn the heart of the fathers to the children and the heart of the children to their fathers, lest I come and smite the earth with a curse."

4-B: CONTENTS OF THE TWENTY SEVEN BOOKS OF THE NEW TESTAMENT, IN BRIEF

The twenty seven books in the New Testament can be grouped into the following four groups:-

I.   THE GOSPELS:

1. *Matthew* 2. *Mark* 3. *Luke* 4. *John*

The term Gospel is an English term "God spell", which means God's news.

The four gospels tell the story of Jesus – his birth, his life, his death on the cross and his resurrection, and ascension to heaven.

The first three gospels (Matthew, Mark and Luke) have similar way to explanation. So, they are known as "Synoptic Gospels." The term "Synoptic" is a Greek term, meaning, "See together." In the Synoptic gospels, Jesus explained to people by telling short parables, whereas in St.John's gospel, Jesus taught people by long statements.

II. HISTORICAL

1. *Acts*

Only one book of Acts is historical. This book tells the history of how the churches were built in different places, and what happened to the early promoters of churches to spread the gospel and the kingdom of God.

III. LETTERS

These are twenty-one letters written mostly by Paul. These letters contain the instructions of Paul to the Christians in different places, as to know how to live as Christians.

1) Romans 2) 1ˢᵗ Corinthians 3) 2ⁿᵈ Corinthians 4) Galatians
5) Ephesians 6) Philippians 7) Colossians 8) 1ˢᵗ Thessalonians
9) 2ⁿᵈ Thessalonians 10) 1ˢᵗ Timothy 11) 2ⁿᵈ Timothy 12) Titus
13) Philemon 14) Hebrews 15) James 16) 1ˢᵗ Peter 17) 2ⁿᵈ Peter
18)1ˢᵗ John 19) 2ⁿᵈ John 20) 3ʳᵈ John 21) Jude

IV. PROPHECY

This book deals with the John's vision of what will happen at
the end of the world.

1. Revelation

All these twenty seven books of the New Testament are
explained in brief in the following pages:-

1. The Gospels

BOOK NO.: 1. MATTHEW

This book was written by Mathew, also called Levi, who was
one of the disciples of Jesus Christ.

Mathew was a tax collector in the Roman government.
When Jesus saw him and called him to follow him as his
disciple, Mathew immediately followed Jesus (Luke 5: 27, 28).

Chapter 1:1 to 17 says that Jesus belonged to the 42nd
generation of Abraham, because from Abraham to David are
fourteen generations, from David to Israelites being carried away
to Babylon are fourteen generations and from carrying away
to Babylon to Jesus are fourteen generations. Chapters 1 and 2
explain the birth of Jesus in Bethlehem during the time of King
Herod and Herod commanding his soldiers to kill all male
children below two years of age, just to kill baby Jesus also.

John the Baptist preaching in the wilderness of Judea,
baptism of Jesus in river Jordan by John the Baptist, Jesus
fasting for forty days and forty nights and later on, temptation
by satan are explained in Chapter three and four.

Seeing the multitude, Jesus went up a mountain and taught them, saying :-

> "Blessed are the poor in spirit; for theirs is the kingdom of heaven etc., etc., like that eight blessings. This is known as "The Sermon on the mount"(Chapter 5:1 to 10).

Chapter 4: 18 to 22 says that as Jesus was walking along the sea of Galilee, he saw Peter, his brother Andrew, James and his brother John, who were catching fish in the sea of Galilee and asked them to follow him as his disciples, and they followed Jesus. Jesus performed two miracles and narrated eleven parables, which are explained at the end of this book as a separate chapter.

Crucification of Jesus in Jerusalem, his resurrection and ascension to heaven are explained in chapters 26 to 28.

BOOK NO.: 2 – MARK

It is believed that this book was written by a man named John Mark, who worked with Peter for many years and Peter told him all about Jesus. It seems that the people in the Roman Empire did not know anything about Jesus and Jews and hence, Mark wrote this book for the knowledge of those in Rome.

Chapters 1 to 9 explain the events that took place in Galilee region and Chapters 10 to 16 explain the events that took place in or near Jerusalem.

Jesus healed a man who could not walk (Chapter 2:1 to 12), - Jesus raised a dead girl (Chapter 5:21 to 43), Jesus calmed a storm on the sea of Galilee (Chapter 4:35 to 41) – Jesus walked on the water of sea of Galilee (Chapter 6:45 to 56) – Jesus fed four thousands people with seven loaves and a few fishes (Chapter 8:1 to 10) – Jesus healed a young boy having dumb spirit (Chapter 9:14 to 32) – Last supper of Jesus with his disciples in the Upper Room (Chapter 14:12 to 26) – Crucifixion of Jesus and placing his body in the rock tomb of Joseph

Arimathia (Chapter 15:21 to 47) - Resurrection of Jesus and ascension to heaven (Chapter 16:1 to 20).

All the miracles performed by Jesus and parables narrated by him are explained under separate chapters at the end of this book.

BOOK NO.: 3 – LUKE

This book was written by Luke, who was a doctor and who travelled with Paul.

In the 1st chapter, the birth of John (John the Baptist later on) to Zachariah a priest and his wife Elisabeth who were very old and righteous people is explained.

In Chapter 2: 1 to 39 the birth of Jesus in Bethlehem and the blessing of Simeon when Jesus was taken to Jerusalem are explained. Simeon sang a song to rejoice, which is now known as "The Nunc Dimittis."

Chapter 3:21 to 23 explain the baptism of Jesus by John the Baptist in river Jordan, when Jesus was thirty years old. Immediately after the baptism, Jesus was led by the Spirit into the wilderness and he spent forty days and forty nights fasting and praying. After that, Jesus was tempted by satan, but Jesus conquered satan (Chapter 4:1 to 13).

Jesus started preaching in Nazareth and all were amazed. While walking along the Sea of Galilee, Jesus chose Simon Peter and his brother Andrew, John and his brother James, who were all fishermen, as his first disciples (Chapter 5:2 to 11).

Chapter 6:12 to 16 says that Jesus went out into a mountain to pray, and continued all night in prayer to God. When it was day, Jesus called his twelve disciples, whose names are:-

1) Simon Peter, 2) Andrew, 3) James, 4) John, 5) Philip, 6) Bartholomew, 7) Matthew, 8) Thomas, 9) James, son of Alphaeus 10) Simon, called Zelotes, 11) Judas, brother of James, 12) Judas Iscariot, who was the traitor of Jesus.

Jesus went to Capernaum and a certain centurion's servant was sick and was about to die. The centurion had great faith in Jesus' healing power and he asked Jesus not to take the trouble of coming to his house, but say a word and his servant shall be healed. Jesus was surprised at his faith and healed his servant (Chapter 7:1 to 10).

Jesus raised the son of a widow though the son was dead and being carried out of the city of Nain (Chapter 7:11 to 15). Thus, Jesus performed many miracles to heal the people of their infirmities, plagues, evil spirits and the blind, etc.

Jesus narrated many parables also like; i) A sower sowing his seed, some of which fell by way side, some on rock and some on good ground, which gave fruit of hundredfold (Chapter 8:4 to 18)., ii) The Parable of a Good Samaritan (Chapter 10: 30 to 37)., iii) The Parable of a rich man, who had plentiful of crop and was extremely happy having procured treasure for himself but not rich towards God and God said to him "thou fool, this night you might die and whose wealth all this be (Chapter 12 :16 to 21), iv) The Parable of Prodigal son (Chapter 15:11 to 32), v) The Story of a rich man and poor Lazarus (Chapter 16:19 to 31), Jesus healed ten lepers (Chapter 17:12 to 19), etc.

Jesus was passing through Jericho, when Zacchaeus desired to see him and climbed up a sycamore tree and Jesus called him down and abided with him for that day (Chapter 19:1 to 10).

Chapter 22 to 24 deals with the crucifixion of Jesus Christ in Jerusalem, his resurrection and his ascension to heaven, telling his disciples to preach repentance and remission of sins in His name among all nations, beginning at Jerusalem. Jesus took his disciples up to Bethany (only three kms. from Jerusalem), lifted up his hands and blessed them. While he was blessing them, he parted from them and was carried up into heaven (Chapter 24:47 to 53).

The most important event in this book is, in Chapter 11:1 to 4, which say, "As he was praying in a certain place, when he ceased, one of his disciples said unto him, Lord, teach us to pray, as John also taught his disciples." Jesus said to his disciples, "When ye pray, say, Our father which art in heaven, Hallowed be thy name. Thy Kingdom come. Thy will be done, as in heaven, so in earth. Give us day by day our daily bread. And forgive us our sins: for we also forgive everyone that is indebted to us. And lead us not into temptation: but deliver us from evil." It is a short and sweet prayer, which is now being used everywhere as "Lord's Prayer."

All the miracles and parables narrated by Jesus are explained under separate chapters at the end of this book.

BOOK NO.: 4 – JOHN

This book was written by John, who was a follower of Jesus.

The book starts by saying, "In the beginning was the word, and the word was with God, and the word was God. All things were made by him; and without him was not anything made that was made."

The mission of John the Baptist and Jesus' baptism in river Jordan by John the Baptist are explained (1:6 to 33). Jesus chose his first disciples (Chapter 1:37 to 51).

Jesus went with his disciples to a wedding in Cana (near Nazareth) and Jesus' mother was also there. When his mother told Jesus that there was no wine, Jesus performed his first miracle of changing water into wine (Chapter 2:1 to 11).

Then, Jesus went to Jerusalem, as it was Jews Passover festival. Jesus was furious to see that people were selling oxen, sheep, and doves and there were moneychangers. Jesus made a scourge of small cords and he drove them all out of the temple saying, "Make not my Father's house a house of merchandise" (Chapter 2:13 to 17).

The Jews asked Jesus what sign he would show, as he was doing all this. Jesus said, "Destroy this temple, and in three days I will raise it up." The Jews said that it took forty-six years to build this temple, but could you build it in three days? – But, Jesus spoke of the temple of his body (which would rise three days after his death) (Chapter 2:18 to 21).

Eight miracles performed by Jesus and many parables narrated by Jesus are recorded in this book. All the miracles performed by Jesus and parables narrated by him have been explained under separate chapters at the end of this book.

Jesus told that he was a good shepherd, and knows his sheep very well (Chapter 10: 1 to 18).

Jesus raised Lazarus, brother of Mary and Martha in Bethany, as he was dead (Chapter 11:1 to 44).

Jesus predicted his death in Jerusalem and told his disciples about it.

Chapters 17 to 21 deal with his last journey to Jerusalem, last supper with his disciples in the Upper room in Jerusalem, his prayer in the garden of Gethsemane, trial before Pontius Pilot, his crucifiction, placing his body in the rock tomb of Joseph Arimathia, his resurrection on the third day and ascension to heaven.

II. HISTORICAL

BOOK NO.: 5 – ACTS

This book was written by Luke, who was a doctor and always followed Paul.

This book deals with the setting up and growth of early churches in different countries during the period after the ascension of Jesus to heaven till the time Paul was imprisoned in Rome, the capital of Italy.

This book can be divided into two parts – 1) Preaching in Jerusalem, and 2) Preaching in places other than Jerusalem. In Jerusalem, the preaching was mainly among the Jews in Jerusalem and Peter was the main person who preached assisted by John. Once, Peter and John went into the temple in Jerusalem and there was a man lame by birth sitting at the gate of the temple and the gate was known as "Beautiful gate." This man was begging every day and when he saw Peter and John, he asked for alms. But, Peter prayed and said to the lame man "Silver and gold have I none, but such as I have give I thee: In the name of Jesus Christ of Nazareth rise up and walk." The lame man started walking and all the people were surprised. Peter preached to them and many were baptized on that day itself. Then, Annas the high priest, Caiaphas, Alexander and many high priests gathered in Jerusalem, called Peter and John and threatened them not to preach in the name of Jesus. Many, who believed in Jesus Christ sold their lands and houses and brought their price to Peter and John and apostles for preaching (Chapters 3 and 4). But, a man by name Ananias sold his land and in consultation with his wife Sapphira brought only a part of the money and laid it at the feet of apostle Peter. Peter rebuked him saying that Ananias had lied unto God. Hearing this, Ananiah fell down there itself and died. The young men carried him and buried. After three hours, his wife Sapphira came not knowing all this. When Peter asked her whether it was all the price of the land that they sold, she said, yes. Peter said, "The feet of those who carried and buried your husband are at the door." She also fell dead. There was a great fear among all people, who saw Anania and Sapphira dying for telling a lie to God (Chapter 5:1 to 11).

More and more believers were bringing sick people to see that at least the shadow of Peter might fall on them and get cured. Seeing all this, the high priest imprisoned the apostles. But, the angel of the Lord opened the doors of the prison and allowed the apostles to come out and again preach in the temple. The high priest and other rulers were surprised as to how they came out of prison, which was properly locked (Chapter 5:12 to 42).

As more and more believers were coming up, the apostles appointed seven honest men to look after the matters. Among the seven men, Stephen was one, a man of full faith. Stephen did great wonders and miracles among people. People set up false witness saying Stephen spoke blasphemous words against the holy place and the law and brought him before the high priest. Stephen was questioned by the high priest, and Stephen told the whole history of how God was with Abraham, Issac, Jacob, Joseph and Moses and how God brought the Israelites from Egypt to Cannan through wilderness for forty years. When the high priest and other rulers heard Stephen, they became furious. But, Stephen being full of the Holy Ghost looked at heaven and said, "Behold, I see the heavens opened and the son of man standing on the right hand of God." Then, the high priest and rulers ran upon Stephen at once. They cast Stephen out of the city of Jerusalem and stoned him to death. All the witnesses laid down their clothes at a young man's feet, whose name was Saul (Chapter 6:1 to 15, 7:1 to 60).

Saul consented to the death of Stephen. He started persecuting Christians and many Christians left Jerusalem and went to Judea, Samaria, etc. Then, Philip went to the city of Samaria and preached Christ to them. He performed many miracles and there was great joy in that city. The angel of the Lord spoke to Philip asking him to go to the way leading from Jerusalem to Gaza. An Ethiopian, who came to worship in Jerusalem, was returning on a chariot, reading the Book of Esaias the prophet. Philip asked him whether he was able to understand what he was reading. The Ethiopian said, "How can I understand, except some man should guide me." Philip went up the chariot and sat with him. The portion he was reading was "He was led as a sheep to the slaughter: and like a lamb dumb before his shearer, so opened he not his mouth." Philip preached to him of Jesus. When the chariot came to a place, where there was water, the Ethiopian asked Philip to baptize him with water and he did so. As they were coming out of water, Philip disappeared from the Ethiopian (Chapter 8:1 to 40).

Chapter 9 is the most important for all Christians as it deals with the conversion of Saul to Christianity.

Saul was persecuting all Christians by entering into every Christian household and putting them into prisons. Saul went to the high priest and took letters to the synagogues in Damascus giving him power to bring the Christians bound to Jerusalem. As he approached Damascus, suddenly there was a bright light around him from heaven. Saul fell to the earth due to the bright light. Saul heard a voice saying, "Saul, Saul, why persecutest thou me?" Saul asked, "Who art thou Lord" And the Lord said, "I am Jesus, whom thou persecutest: it is hard for thee to kick against the pricks." Saul was astonished and trembling said, "Lord, what wilt thou have me to do?" The Lord said, "Arise, and go into the city, and it shall be told thee what thou must do." The men who were with Saul stood speechless, as they heard the voice but saw no man. Saul became blind and so, the men had to guide him by hand and brought him to Damascus city. Saul was blind for three days and he neither ate nor drank.

At Damascus, there was a disciple by name, Ananias who had a vision in which the Lord asked him to go to the house of Judah, where Saul was staying blind. Saul also had a vision in which a man by name Ananias came and placed his hands on Saul to receive his sight. Ananias answered the Lord, saying that Saul had done evil to the saints in Jerusalem and he had come to Damascus to bind all those who call the Lord's name. But the Lord said, "Saul was his chosen person to speak about him to gentiles, kings and the children of Israel, and so he should meet Saul." Ananias went accordingly and entered the house, placed his hands on Saul, and said, "Brother Saul, the Lord, even Jesus, that appeared unto thee in the way as thou camest, hath sent me, that thou mightest receive thy sight, and be filled with the Holy Ghost." Immediately scales fell from his eyes and Saul received sight and was baptized. After eating, he was strengthened and started preaching in the synagogues, saying Christ is the Son of God. But those who heard him were amazed and plotted to kill Saul. The disciples took him in a night and let him down the city walls in a basket. Saul came to Jerusalem and desired to be with the disciples. But, they did not believe Saul. Barnabas told all the apostles that Saul had a vision on way to Damascus and he was now the disciple of Jesus Christ. The Grecians were furious and wanted to kill Saul. When the brethren heard of this plot, they brought Saul to Caesarea and sent him to Tarsus.

Chapter 9:32 to 43 says that Peter went to all places preaching and came to Lydda. There was a person known as Aeneas sick of palsy for eight years. Apostle Peter said, "Aeneas, in the name of Jesus Christ, arise." He was healed and all people at Lydda and Saron turned towards the Lord.

At Joppa, there was a disciple by name Tabitha, who was also known as Dorcas. She was full of good works. She fell ill and died. Joppa was near Lydda, where apostle Peter was staying. When the people at Joppa heard of Peter, they sent men to bring Peter, who came and prayed and Tabitha rose up. Many people at Joppa also believed in the Lord.

Chapter 10, explains how Cornelius, a centurion at a place known as Caesarea and many others turned to the Lord. Cornelius was a very god fearing person, though he was a very high official, as centurion of Italian band. One day, he saw a vision in which the Lord asked him to send men to Joppa and bring Peter, who was staying in the house of another person by name Peter, who was a tanner and hear him. Two men sent by Cornelius were drawing near to the house of Simon the tanner in Joppa. Just at that time, Apostle Peter went up to the housetop to pray. As he was hungry, he fell asleep. He saw a vision in which the heaven opened and certain vessel descending unto him. In that, Peter saw all kinds of four footed beasts, creeping things and fowls of the air. A voice came saying, "Rise, Peter, kill and eat." Peter answered, "Not so Lord, for I have never eaten anything that is common or unclean." The voice came a second time saying, "What God hath cleansed, that call not thou common." The voice came a third time and the vessel was received up again into heaven. Peter was thinking what this vision meant. He was told by Simon the tanner that three men came seeking him. Next morning, Apostle Peter went with the three men to Caesarea to meet Cornelius of whom he heard from these three men. When Apostle Peter was entering the house, Cornelius fell down at Peter's feet and worshipped him. But, Peter took him up saying that he was also a man. Cornelius, being a Jew and a centurion invited many people into his house so that they could all hear Peter. By knowing that there were many other than Jews also whom Cornelius invited, Peter felt in his heart that the vision he had on the housetop of Simon the tanner made him realize that he should not call any man common or unclean. Cornelius told apostle Peter the vision he had and how he sent men to Joppa to invite him. Peter preached to all of them about Jesus Christ as Jesus' commanded him to preach unto the people. As Peter was speaking, the Holy Ghost fell on all and they spoke in tongues praising God. Peter baptized all of them and they asked Peter to stay with them for a few days.

Chapter 11 explains that Apostle Peter came to Jerusalem and narrated the entire story, as to how he went to Cornelius and baptized many. They were happy and glorified God. Preaching was carried out in Phenice, Cyprus and Antioch.

Chapter 12 says that in order to please the people, King Herod killed James, the brother of John. Herod wanted to kill Apostle Peter also, but as they were the days of unleavened bread, Herod kept Peter in prison and asked the prison keeper to bring Peter to him after Easter. Peter was praying continuously. Peter was sleeping between the two soldiers in the prison, bound with two chains and the soldiers were also at the door of the prison. That night, the angel of the Lord came upon Peter and woke him up and led him through the four gates, which opened on their own accord and brought Peter to a street in Jerusalem and vanished. Peter realized God's help in rescuing him from the hands of Herod and went into the house of Mary, the mother of John, where many believers gathered to pray. When Peter knocked the door, they opened it and were surprised to see Peter, who was in prison. Peter asked them to be silent and from there, he went elsewhere. Next morning, Herod was surprised as to how Peter escaped from the prison and he killed all the keepers of the prison. On an appointed day, Herod with his royal robes sat on the throne and made an oration to the people. Immediately, the angel of the Lord smote Herod, because he gave not God the glory: and Herod was eaten by worms and died.

Chapter 13 deals with the preaching's of apostles in different countries. In chapter 13:9, it is said that Saul (who also is called Paul) cursed a sorcerer by name Elymus for trying to desuade a believer and he became blind. From here onwards, in all other chapters, the name Paul is mentioned in place of Saul. The twenty one epistles are said to have been mostly written by Paul. Silas and Paul went to Macedonia to preach. A woman by name Lydia was baptized and accommodated Paul and Silas in her house for a few days. When they were praying there, a girl possessed by an evil spirit came along with her master, a soothsayer. Paul prayed and drove out the evil spirit. But, the soothsayer was angry and took Paul and Silas to magistrates saying that these two men were Jews and doing acts not suitable to Romans. All people rose against Paul and Silas and after beating them, with the orders of the magistrate, Paul and Silas were kept in a prison. But at night, there was an earthquake and the foundations of prison were shaken and the prison doors were opened. The prison keeper thought that Paul and Silas might have fled and tried to kill himself with his sword. But, Paul cried out saying do not harm yourself, as we are in prison. The keeper of the jail fell on Paul's feet and he was baptized. Next morning, the magistrates allowed them to go away. Then, Paul went to Thessalonica, Athens, Corinth, Cyria and returned to Caesarea. Then, Paul travelled by ships to many places.

Finally, Paul was brought before King Agrippa in Caesarea. Paul was asked to speak. Paul told them how he was earlier persecuting Christians and how he became a Christian, when he saw a vision on way to Damascus. All of them found no fault in Paul. So, they allowed Paul to sail with others to Rome (Italy) to be presented before Caesar, the Emperor of Rome at that time. While Paul was sailing with others, there was storm on the sea and the life of those in the ship was in danger. Paul prayed continuously and told all the passengers on the ship that not a hair shall fall from their head as God was with them all. After fourteen days of fasting in the fear of life, they were cheered up by the encouraging words of Paul and all of them ate bread. At last after some days, the ship landed on an unknown island. The people living on that small and remote island were barbarous. But, peculiarly, they were very kind to those shipwrecked people who were with Paul. As it was very cold, they kindled a fire to warm them. Paul gathered a bundle of sticks and lighted it. A venomous snake came out of the kindled sticks and fastened to the hand of Paul. Everyone in that island thought that he was a sinner and he would die by the snakebite. But, Paul shook it off from his hand without getting panicky and the snake fell down without biting Paul. All the natives of that island were surprised and realized that Paul was a man of God. Paul healed many sick people on that island and the natives were grateful to Paul. They allowed all the shipwrecked passengers to sail again in the ship towards Rome, giving them lot of food for their journey. At last, after many months of sailing the ship reached Rome. All the passengers were kept in a prison, but Paul was allowed to reside with a soldier. From there, Paul preached to many, some believing and some not believing. Paul stayed there for two years.

Then, Paul wrote fourteen epistles, explaining about his deep devotion to Christ, his experiences in prisons, Christ's second coming etc. to the believers in different countries like Corinth, Galatia, Ephesus, Philippi, Colosse, Thessalonica, etc.

BOOK NO.: 6 – ROMANS

This epistle was written by Paul to Romans.

In all these epistles, Paul starts by saying, "Paul, a servant of Jesus Christ, called to be an apostle, Grace be unto you and peace from the Lord, Jesus Christ."

Paul wrote this epistle when he was living in Corinth. Paul greeted all Christians in Rome and expressed his desire to visit Rome and preach to all. Paul said to them that Christ being raised from the dead dieth no more and death had no more domain over him. Likewise, everyone should consider them to be dead unto sin, but alive unto God through Jesus Christ our Lord. Paul said that the wages of sin were death, but the gift of God is eternal life through Jesus Christ, our Lord.

Paul stressed that all mankind, both Jews and gentiles, need to be put right with God, as all are under the power of sin. This can be done by having faith in our Lord, Jesus Christ. Paul also said that a believer has peace with God and is set free by God's spirit from the power of sin and death. Paul discussed the purpose of the Law of God and the power of God's spirit in a believer's life. Paul said that the rejection of Jesus Christ by the Jews and gentiles fits into the plan of God for mankind. Paul concluded by saying that the rejection of Jesus Christ is within God's plan and firmly believed that Jews will not always reject Jesus Christ. Paul wrote about how Christians should love one another. Paul sent his personal greetings to everyone living in Rome. He advised all of them to salute the believers of Jesus Christ and greet one another with a holy kiss, as the church of Christ saluted them all. Finally, Paul wrote that the God of Peace shall bruise satan under its feet shortly and the Grace of our Lord Jesus Christ is with them all.

BOOK NO. : 7 – I CORINTHIANS

This is the first epistle of Paul to the Christians living in Corinth. Earlier, Paul had established a church there.

Paul wrote, saying that "I heard of divisions among you. Some say, that I am of Paul, and some say I am of Apollos, some say I am of Cephas, and some say I am of Christ. Is Christ divided? Was Paul crucified for you? Or were ye baptized in the name of Paul? I thank God that I had not baptized anyone of you except a few, for Christ sent me not to baptize, but to preach the gospel. Who is Paul and who is Apollos? They are ministers of God by whom ye believed. I have planted, Apollos watered, but God made it grow. They are all one in God and every man shall receive his reward according to his own labour."

Paul wrote in this epistle, "It is reported to me that there is fornication (adultery) among you. Flee from fornication. He that committeth fornication sinneth against his own body. Your body is the temple of the Holy Ghost, which is in you, which ye have of God, and ye are your own. For ye are bought with a price; therefore glorify God in your body, and in your spirit, which are God's" (Chapter 5:1 and 6:18 to 20).

In Chapter 11:3 to 9, it is said that Paul wrote to Corinthians saying, "I want you to know that the head of every man is Christ: and the head of a woman is a man and the head of Christ is God. Every man praying or prophesying, having his head covered, dishonoureth his head (Christ). Every woman that prayeth or prophesieth with her head uncovered dishonoureth her head (a man) for that is even all one as if she were shaven. A man indeed ought not to cover his head, for as much as he is the image and glory of God: but the woman is the glory of the man. For the man is not of the woman: but the woman is of the man. Neither the man was created for the woman, but the woman for the man."

In Chapter 13:1 to 13 Paul wrote about charity saying, "Charity suffered long, and is kind : charity envieth not:

charity vaunteth not itself, is not puffed up. When I was a child, I spoke as a child, I understood as a child : but when I became a man, I put away childish things. And now abideth faith, hope and charity, these three: but the greatest of these is charity."

In Chapter 16:1 to 24, Paul wrote concerning collection of funds for the saints. He wrote that on the first day of the week, let every one of you lay aside what God hath prospered him and he would send some one to collect their free will offerings. Finally, Paul greeted all of them and blessed them in the name of our Lord Jesus Christ.

BOOK NO.: 8 – II CORINTHIANS

This is the second epistle of Paul to the Christians living in Corinth.

Paul thanked the Lord for helping him in all troubles. He expressed his love for all Christians at Corinth, though some opposed him. But, Paul advised all to love such people also and make them realize their mistakes.

Chapter 1:8 to 11 says that when he was in Asia, they were in great trouble, but God saved them. So, Paul thanked all those who prayed for them.

Paul pleaded with them to love those who caused grief to them (Chapter 2:5 to 11). Paul pleaded with the believers in Corinth to donate liberally for the service of God. Paul said, "He which soweth sparingly shall reap also sparingly; and he which soweth bountifully shall reap also bountifully. Every man, according as he purposeth in his heart, so let him give; not grudgingly, or of necessity; for God loveth a cheerful giver" (Chapter 9:5 to 7).

Paul made a personal appeal to all in Corinth saying that he was kind to them when he is with them and he is harsh when he is away from them. He said, "We destroy false arguments and we make everyone obey Christ. Who so ever wants to boast must boast about what he, Lord had done."

Paul cautioned all of them about false apostles, who lie about their work and disguise themselves to look like real apostles of Christ, as satan also can disguise himself to look like an angel of light (Chapter 11:12 to 14).

Paul told them all his sufferings as an apostle. He said, "I was in prison many times. I was whipped many times. I had been near death many times. Five times I was given thirty-nine lashes by Jews, three times I was whipped by Romans and once I was stoned. I was shipwrecked thrice and I was in water for twenty-four hours. I had no food, no shelter and no sleep many times. When I was in Damascus, the King Aretas placed guards at all the city gates to arrest me, but I was let down by believers in a basket through a window outside the city wall and I escaped his hands."

Paul revealed his great concern for all the Corinthians. Finally, Paul warned them against sin and advised them to strive for perfection, live in peace so that, God of love and peace will be with them.

BOOK NO.: 9 – GALATIANS

This epistle was written by Paul to Christians in Galatia, a Roman province in Asia Minor.

Paul was surprised to observe that the people in Galatia to whom he preached about Jesus Christ just a few days back have lost their faith, due to the preaching's of false apostles. Paul said that the gospel, which he preached to them, is not after man, as he neither received it of man, but it was the revelation of Jesus Christ.

In Chapter 6:10 to 18 Paul pleaded with Galatians to do good unto all men, especially unto them who are of the household of faith. Paul blessed them all and said, "From hence forth let no man trouble me : for I bear in my body the marks of the Lord Jesus. Grace of our Lord Jesus Christ be with your spirit."

BOOK NO.: 10 – EPHESIANS

Paul wrote this epistle to the saints and to the faithful in Christ Jesus living in Ephesus.

The church in Ephesus was getting divided as the converted Jews in the early churches were trying to be separate from the gentile Christians. Paul pleaded with them all to be united into one body for the indwelling of the Holy Spirit.

Chapters 5:22 to 25, Paul advised the wives to submit themselves to unto their husbands as unto the Lord. For the husband is the head of the wife, even as Christ is the head of the church and is the saviour of the body. Paul also advised the husbands to love their wives, even as Christ also loved the church and gave himself for it. Paul, in Chapter 6:1 to 6, advised the children to obey their parents in the Lord for this is right. He asked the children to honour their father and mother (which is the first commandment of the Lord) so that, they may live long on the earth. Paul advised the fathers also not to provoke their children to wrath : but bring them up in the nurture and admonition of the Lord. Paul advised the servants to be obedient to them that are masters. Paul advised the masters also to be kind to their servants. Paul advised all to put on the armour of God, that ye may be able to stand against the wiles of the devils. Paul concluded this epistle by blessing them saying, "Grace be with all them that love our Lord Jesus Christ in sincerity."

BOOK NO.: 11 – PHILIPPIANS

This epistle was written by Paul saying, "Paul and Timotheus, the servants of Jesus Christ, to all the saints in Christ Jesus, which are at Philippi, with the bishops and deacons, Grace be to you and peace from God our Father, and from the Lord Jesus Christ."

Paul wrote (Chapter 2: 5 to 11), "Let the mind of Christ be in you, who being in the form of God, thought it not robbery to be equal with God, but made himself of no reputation and took upon him the form of a servant, and was made in the likeness of men: And being found in fashion as a man, he humbled himself, and became obedient unto death, even the death on the cross. Therefore, God also hath highly exalted him, and given him a name which is above every name : That in the name of Jesus, every knee should bow, of things in heaven, and things in earth, and things under the earth. And every tongue should confess that Jesus Christ is the Lord, to the glory of God the Father. Do all things without murmuring and disputing and shine as lights in the world."

Finally, Paul prayed for all of them saying, "The peace of God, which passeth all understanding shall keep your hearts and minds through Jesus Christ, The Grace of our Lord Jesus Christ be with you all."

BOOK NO.: 12 – COLOSSIANS

This epistle was written by Paul along with Timotheus to the saints and faithful brethren in Christ living in Colosse, a city of Asia minor.

Paul wrote, "You have faith in Christ Jesus and you have love to all saints. Do not be convinced by any enticing words of any man. For though I be absent in the flesh yet am I with you in the spirit, joying and beholding your order and steadfastness of your faith in Christ. As ye have therefore received Christ Jesus the Lord, so walk ye in him."

Paul advised wives, husbands, children, fathers and servants to love one another, as he wrote earlier to people in Philippines. Paul sent his greetings and those of other saints that were working with him.

BOOK NO.: 13 – I THESSALONIANS

Paul in his first epistle to the church of the Thessalonians greeted them all along with Silvanus and Timotheus, who were with him.

There was opposition from Jews, who were jealous of Paul's success in preaching the gospel among non-Jews, who had become interested in Judaism. Paul had to leave Thessalonica but sent Timothy to encourage them in their faith. Timothy returned to Paul, who was in Athens and brought good news of the continuing faith of them in Thessalonica. Paul was happy to hear about the faith of the believers in Thessalonica, their charity and their anxiety to see each other.

In Chapter 4, Paul advised them all to lead a life without sin, and love one another and all those in Macedonia. Paul said that the Lord himself will descend from heaven with a shout, with the voice of archangel and with the trumpet of God and the dead in Christ will rise first.

In Chapter 5, Paul advised them all to be at peace among themselves, and do their own business and work with their own hands, so that they may lack nothing. He advised them to rejoice always, pray without ceasing and in everything give thanks, for this is the will of God in Christ Jesus for them. He also advised them not to despise prophecies, hold fast what is good and abstain from every form of evil, so that the God of Peace sanctify them wholly. Paul finally advised them to pray for him, greet all brethren with a holy kiss and read this epistle to all holy brethren. He blessed them with the grace of our Lord Jesus Christ.

BOOK NO.: 14 – II THESSALONIANS

This second epistle was also written by Paul to all the believers in Thessalonica. Paul greeted them on behalf of Silvanus and Timothy. Paul wrote, saying that, "he was boasting of the believers in Thessalonica among all churches of God, for their patience, and faith in all their persecutions and tribulations that they were enduring. But, God will punish all those who are against you, when he comes with his mighty angels, and is flaming fire to take vengeance on those who do not know God and those who do not obey the gospel of our Lord Jesus Christ. Paul said that he was praying always that the God should count them worthy of his calling."

In Chapter 2, Paul asked all in Thessalonica not to believe false prophets, who say that the day of the Lord has already come. Paul asked them to stand firm and hold to the teachings of our Lord Jesus Christ.

Finally, Paul asked them to pray for him, so that, the message of the Lord may spread rapidly and be honoured as it was with them. Paul further advised them not to keep company with any man, who is idle. If a man is not working, he shall not eat, should be the principle. Paul finally greeted them in the name of our Lord Jesus Christ.

BOOK NO.: 15 – I TIMOTHY

This is a personal letter of Paul to Timothy, whom he called his true son in faith.

Paul warned Timothy to stop certain people teaching false doctrine, which promote controversies rather than God's work, which is by faith.

Paul wrote saying that once he was a persecutor, and a violent man. But, the grace of the Lord was poured on him so that the unlimited patience of Jesus might be displayed through a sinner.

Paul desired (Chapter 2:1 to 11) that every man should lift up his hands in prayer without anger or disputing. Paul advised all women to dress modestly and learn to be quiet and submissive.

In Chapter 3, Paul prescribed qualifications of bishops,

deacons. Paul advised the elders, younger men and women should be treated with all respect. He also advised how widows should behave and advised all to give proper recognition to those widows who are really in need.

In Chapter 6, Paul wrote by saying that if any man has love for money without contentment, it is bad, for we brought nothing into the world and we take nothing out of it. But, if we have food and clothing, we will be content with that. People, who want to get rich fall into temptation and will fall into destruction. For the love for money is the root cause of all kinds of evil.

Paul advised Timothy to flee from all this and pursue righteousness, godliness, faith, love, endurance and gentleness.

BOOK NO.: 16 –II TIMOTHY

Paul wrote the second epistle also to Timothy and said that the strong faith in him was first in his grandmother, Lois and in his mother Eunice, and then, in him.

Paul advised Timothy to be strong in the grace that is in Christ Jesus. Paul advised Timothy not to be ashamed of the gospel nor him, for we know whom we have believed and are persuaded that He is able to keep what we have committed to Him until that day.

In Chapter 2, Paul advised Timothy to endure hardship as a good soldier of Jesus Christ. Paul also advised Timothy to flee from youthful lusts, but pursue righteousness, faith, love, and peace with those who call on the Lord out of a pure heart. Avoid foolish and ignorant disputes knowing that they generate strife. Paul advised that a servant of the Lord must not quarrel but be gentle to all, able to teach patience. Chapter 3:16 say, "All scripture is given by inspiration of God."

In Chapter 4, Paul said that the time of his departure was at hand. He had fought the good fight and finished the race and kept the faith. Paul was awaiting the crown of

Righteousness, which the Lord, the righteous judge will give to him on that day and not to him alone, but to all who loved Him. Finally, Paul sent his greetings to all believers.

BOOK NO.: 17 – TITUS

This epistle was written by Paul to Titus, who was earlier a Greek and converted to Christianity by Paul and was assisting Paul in the gospel work in Crete.

In Chapter 1, Paul mentioned about the qualities of elders. He said that a bishop must be blameless as a steward of God, not self-willed, not quick tempered, not given to wine, not violent, not greedy for money, but hospitable, a lover of what is good, sober minded, just, holy, self-controlled. Paul mentioned that one of their own Prophets in Crete said, "The people in Crete (Cretans) are always liars, evil beasts, lazy gluttons." Paul said that this testimony is true, so he said that Titus should rebuke them sharply, that they may be sound in the faith.

In Chapter 2, Paul advised Titus to see that the older men should be sober, temperate, sound in faith, and sound in love and patience. Likewise, the older women should be teachers of good things, obedient to their husbands. Young men should be sober minded.

Finally, Paul advised Titus regarding Christian conduct, especially the need to be peaceful, friendly, and to avoid hatred, arguments, and divisions in the church. Paul sent his greetings and greetings of all those believers who were with him.

BOOK NO.: 18 – PHILEMON

Paul wrote this epistle to Philemon, a wealthy slave owner, but a good believer in Christ, residing in Colosse. All the believers were meeting in his house. A slave by name Onesimus was working with Philemon, but he ran away after committing a crime. But Onesimus met Paul in Rome and was converted to Christianity and was helping Paul in the gospel work. So, Paul had a kind heart towards Onesimus. In this epistle, Paul pleaded with Philemon to take back Onesimus, as he was not a mere slave, but a dear brother in Christ. Paul also mentioned that if Onesimus owes anything, Paul would pay it. Finally, Paul sent his greetings and greetings of Epaphras, his fellow prisoner and other fellow labourers like Mark, Aristarchus, Demas, and Luke.

BOOK NO.: 19 – HEBREWS

The correct author of this book is doubtful. Some scholars say that it was written by Paul himself and some say that it was written by Paul's associates like Barnabas or Apollos. This was written to the Christians including Jewish Christians and all other Christians.

The Hebrew Christians were facing oppositions and were about to lose their Christian faith.

In Chapter 1, the author has written that Jesus Christ is above all Prophets, as he sat down on the right hand of the Majesty on high. He is above all angels as it is said, "Thou art my son, this day have I begotten thee. Jesus is a real human being and we must believe Jesus. The blood of Jesus washes away sins. Jesus Christ is the same yesterday and today and forever (Chapter 13:8). Be not carried about with divers and strange doctrines. For it is a good thing that the heart be established with grace, not with meats."

BOOK NO.: 20 – JAMES

The author of this book is uncertain but scholars believe that James himself wrote this book. This book was written to all those Jewish converts living in the entire Roman Empire.

The author said that if any man lacks wisdom let him ask God in faith, as God gives liberally to any person who asks him. The author also said that blessed is the man that endureth temptation, for he is tried and he shall receive the crown of life. God chose the poor people of this world but who are rich in faith. Body without the spirit is dead. Similarly, faith without works is also dead. In Chapter 3, he said that tongue is the fire, as it defileth the whole body. Every kind of beast can be tamed by mankind, but tongue cannot be tamed, as it is an unruly evil, full of deadly poison. Out of the same mouth proceedeth blessing, as well as cursing.

In Chapter 4, the author said, "If any among you is afflicted, let him pray. If any one is merry let him sing psalms. If any one among you is sick, let him call for the elders of the church: and let them pray over him, anointing him with oil in the name of the Lord : And the prayer of faith shall save the sick, and the Lord shall raise him up: and if he has committed sins, they shall be forgiven him. Confess your faults one to another, and pray one for another, that ye may be healed. The effectual fervent prayer of a righteous man availeth much. Elias was a man like us. But with his prayer, he stopped the rain for three years and six months and again, with prayer alone he brought rain and the earth brought forth her fruit."

BOOK NO.: 21 – I PETER

This Epistle was written by Peter, a disciple of Jesus Christ. This was meant for those Christians, who had fled from Nero's persecutions and had taken refuge in Pontus, Galatia, Cappadocia, Asia Minor and Bithynia.

The main objective of this epistle was to inspire and encourage the believers amidst their tribulations and persecutions. Peter said that all flesh was as grass and all the glory of a man as a flower of the grass. The grass withereth and the flower thereof falleth away. But, the word of the Lord endureth forever. And this is the word, which by the gospel is preached unto you. Peter said honour all men, love the brotherhood, fear God, honour the king. Peter advised all servants to be obedient to their masters. He advised wives to be in subjection to their own husbands, as Sarah obeyed her husband, Abraham. He also advised husbands to honour their wives. Finally, he advised all to be of one mind, having compassion on one another, love as brethren, be pitiful, and be courageous. Peter advised the youngsters to submit themselves to the elders and be clothed with humility, for God resisteth the proud and giveth grace to the humble. Peter therefore said humble yourself under the mighty hand of God so that, he might exhalt you in due time. Finally, Peter sent greetings from all those believers at Babylon.

BOOK NO.: 22 – II PETER

This epistle was also written by Peter to Jewish Christians, who lived in many parts of the Roman Empire.

Peter warned all these believers to be aware of corrupt teachers, like false prophets, who deny the Lord that brought them up and thereby bring about their own fast destruction. Peter said that this second epistle is to stir up their pure minds by way of remembrance. Peter also said that one day with the Lord is like thousand years and a thousand years as one day. The day of the Lord will come as a thief in the night. We, according to his promise, look for new heavens and a new earth, wherein dwelleth righteousness (Chapter 3:13). He finally said, "Grow in grace, and in the knowledge of our Lord and Saviour, Jesus Christ. To him be glory both now and forever."

BOOK NO.: 23 – I JOHN

This epistle was written by John, who was a disciple of Jesus Christ. This epistle was written for all Christians.

John wrote this epistle to make all believers cheerful. In Chapter 1:6 to 10, John said, "If we say that we have no sin, we deceive ourselves, and the truth is not in us. If we confess our sins, God is just to forgive us our sins, and to cleanse us from all unrighteousness. If we say that we have not sinned, we make him a liar, and his word is not in us."

In Chapter 2:1 to 29 John said, "If any man sin, we have an advocate with the Father, Jesus Christ, the righteous. He is the propitiation of our sins: and not for us only, but also for the sins of the whole world. Anyone who claims to be in the light but, hates his brother is still in darkness. Don't love the world or anything in the world. If anyone loves the world, the love of the Father is not in him. We are approaching the last days, as anti-Christ is coming and trying to lead you astray. Do not let anyone lead you astray. No one, who is born of God will continue in sin, because God's seed remain in him."

John said (Chapter 4:7 to 21), "We should love one another. Anyone, who hates his brother is like Cain, who murdered his own brother and such people have no eternal life in them. We ought to lay down our lives for our brothers, as Jesus Christ laid down His life for all of us. Let us not love one another with mere words or tongue, but love with actions and in truth."

In Chapter 3:1 to 21, John said, "God's command is to believe in the name of his son, Jesus Christ and to love one another. Whosoever loves God must also love his brothers." Finally, John advised all of them to keep away from idols.

BOOK NO.: 24 – II JOHN

This epistle also was written by John the disciple of Jesus Christ to all Christians.

John once again stressed that we should all love one another. He also advised that we should not accommodate any one, who is anti-Christ.

BOOK NO.: 25 – III JOHN

This short epistle was written by John the disciple of Jesus Christ to his dear friend, Gaius, of whom John heard many good things. John was happy to hear from some brethren who told him Gaius's truth that is in him. John said that Diotrephes was not at all helpful and casteth believers out of the church.

But, Demetrius, on the other hand is very helpful. John advised Gaius not to follow that which is evil, but follow that which is good: but he that doeth good is of God : and he that doeth evil hath not seen God.

BOOK NO.: 26 – JUDE

This epistle was written by Jude, a younger brother of James. This epistle was meant for all Christians.

Jude said, "Some Godless men have entered you and they are grumblers and fault finders. They follow their own desires, boast about themselves and flatter others for their own advantage. So, build yourself up in your most holy faith and pray in the Holy Spirit. Keep yourselves in God's love as you wait for the mercy of our Lord Jesus Christ to bring you to eternal life."

BOOK NO.: 27 – REVELATION

This is the last book, out of the twenty seven books in the New Testament.

This book was written by apostle John, when he was in the island of Patmos on the western coast of Asia minor, where he was banished for preaching of Jesus Christ. This letter was addressed by John to seven churches in, 1) Ephesus, 2) Smyrna, 3) Pergamum, 4) Thystira, 5) Sardis 6) Philadelphia, and 7) Laodicea, all in Asia. John wrote, "I was in the isle that is called Patmos. I was in the Spirit on the Lord's day, and heard behind me a great voice, as of a trumpet, saying, I was Alpha and Omega, the first and the last : and what thou seest, write in a book and send it unto the seven churches which are in Asia. And I turned to see the voice that spoke with me. And being turned, I saw seven golden candlesticks. And in the midst of the seven candlesticks, one like unto the son of man, clothed with a garment down to the foot, and girt about the paps with a golden girdle. In his right hand, there were seven stars and out of his mouth came a sharp double-edged sword. His face was like the sun shining. On seeing this vision, John fell down, but the person whom he saw in the vision raised him up saying, "Do not be afraid. I am Alpha and Omega, the first and the last. Write what you are seeing now. The seven stars are the angels of the seven churches and the seven lamp stands are the seven churches."

In the scrolls sent by John to each of these seven churches, the Lord praised in the beginning their faithfulness and love but pointed out their shortcomings and asked them to overcome these shortcomings. At the end of each scroll, it is mentioned that, "He who has an ear, let him hear what the spirit says to each church."

John again heard a voice asking him to come up into the heaven. There, John saw a throne on which someone shining was sitting. Round this throne, there were twenty four thrones and on them twenty four elders were seated. Before these thrones, seven lamps were burning, which were the seven spirits of God. In the center around the throne, there were four living creatures, which were covered with eyes in front and back. The first living creature was like a lion, the second like an ox, the third like a man and the fourth was like a flying eagle. Each of these four living creatures had six wings and were covered with eyes all around, even under their wings. Day and night, these four living creatures were saying, "Holy, holy, holy is the Lord God Almighty, who was and is and is to come." Whenever these four living creatures start singing, the twenty four elders fall down and worship Him, who lives forever.

Then, John saw in the right hand of Him, who sat on the throne, a scroll with writings on both sides and sealed with seven seals. An angel proclaimed, "Who is worthy to break the seals and open the scroll." He fell down and wept. But, one elder raised him up and said, "Do not weep. The lion of the tribe of Judah is able to break the seals and open the scroll." Then, he saw a lamb with seven horns and seven eyes, which are the seven spirits of God sent out into all earth. He came and took the book out of the right hand of him that sat upon the throne. When he had taken the book, the four beasts and twenty four elders fell down before the lamb, having every one of them harps, and golden vials full of odours, which are the prayers of saints. And they sang a new song, saying, "Thou art worthy to take the book, and to open the seals thereof : for thou wast slain, and hast redeemed us to God by thy blood out of every kindred, and tongue, and people and nation." He beheld and heard the voices of many angels round about the throne and the four beasts and twenty four elders : and the number of them was ten thousand times ten thousands, and thousands of thousands. Saying with loud voice, "Worthy is the Lamb that was slain to receive power, and riches, and wisdom, and strength, and honour, and glory, and blessing. And all creatures in heaven, earth heard I saying, "Blessing, and honour, and glory and power, be unto into him that sitteth upon the throne, and unto the Lamb for ever and ever." The four beasts said, "Amen." The twenty four elders fell down and worshipped him that lived forever and ever (Chapter 5: 1 to 14).

Chapter 6:1 to 17 says that John saw, when the Lamb opened one of the seals, John heard a noise like a thunder and one of the four beasts saying, "Come and see." When John saw, a white horse and he that sat on the horse with a bow and a crown was given unto him : and he went forth conquering, and to conquer. As the Lamb opened the remaining six seals one after the other, John saw different peculiar visions. When the sixth seal was opened, there was a great earthquake, the sun turned black and moon turned like blood and the stars of heaven fell on earth, heaven departed as a scroll and every mountain and island were moved out of their places. Every mighty man hid themselves in the dens and in the rocks of the mountain and said to the mountains and rocks, "Fall on us, and hide us from the face of him that sitteth on the throne, and from the wrath of the Lamb. For the great day of his wrath is come : and who shall be able to stand?"

Chapter 7:1 to 17 says that after all this John saw four angels standing on the four corners of the earth, holding the four winds of the earth, that the wind should not blow on the earth, nor on the sea, nor on any tree. John saw another angel ascending from the east, having the seal of the living God : and he cried with a loud voice to the four angels, to whom it was given to hurt the earth and the sea. This angel said, "Hurt not the earth, neither the sea, nor the trees, till we have sealed the servants of our God in their foreheads." Then, from the 12 tribes of Israel, a few thousand people were chosen as servants of God and a seal was put on their foreheads. Thus, this seal was put on a total of 144,000 servants of God. Thus, he saw a great number of servants of God stood before the throne and before the Lamb, clothed with white robes and palms in their hands. They cried with a loud voice, "Salvation to our God, which sitteth upon the throne and unto the Lamb." All the angels stood round about the throne and about the twenty four elders and four beasts who fell upon their faces and worshipped God. One of the elders said that those with white robes are those which came out of great tribulation and have washed their robes and made them white in the blood of the Lamb. Therefore, they are before the throne of God and they serve him day and night in his temple. They shall hunger or thirst no more. The Lamb shall feed them and shall lead them unto the living fountains of water : and God shall wipe away all tears from their eyes.

In Chapter 8:1 to 13 and Chapter 9, it is said that when the seventh seal was opened, there was silence in heaven for half an hour. He saw seven angels standing before the God were given seven trumpets. Another angel with a golden censer came and stood at the altar. The angel took the censer and filled it with fire of the altar and cast it into the earth: and there were voices and thundering and lightning's and an earthquake. The seven angels started sounding the trumpets one after the other and many wonders took place on earth.

Chapter 10 says that he saw another mighty angel coming down from heaven holding a scroll open. His right foot was on the sea and left foot on the land. A voice from heaven was heard asking him to go and take the scroll from the angel. The angel said to him to take the scroll and eat it and it will be sweet like honey in my mouth and it will turn your stomach sour. It happened like that when he ate the scroll. He was told to prophesy again before many people, nations and kings.

Chapter 11 says that he will give power to my two witnesses and they shall prophesy for one hundred twenty six days clothed in sackcloth. These are the two olive trees and the candlesticks standing before God of the earth. If any man will hurt them, fire proceedeth out of their mouth and devoureth their enemies. Verses 15 to 19 says that when the seventh angel sounded the trumpet, loud voice from heaven was heard and the twenty four elders fell on their faces before God, singing in praise of the God.

Chapter 12 says that many wonderous signs appeared in heaven. A woman clothed with the sun and with moon under her feet and a crown of twelve stars on her head. She was about to give birth to a child. A red dragon with seven heads and ten horns and seven crowns on its head stood in front of the woman to devour her new born child. She gave birth to a male child and the child was snatched upto God and to his throne. The woman fled into wilderness, with two wings of a great eagle. The dragon was angry with the woman and went to make war with the remnant of her seed, which keep the commandments of God, and have the testimony of Jesus Christ.

Chapter 13 says that he then stood upon the sand of the sea and saw a beast rise up out of the sea, having seven heads and ten horns and upon his horns, ten crowns and upon his heads the name of blasphemy. The dragon gave the beast his power and his throne and great authority. All men were scared of the beast and dragon and worshipped them. Then, another beast came from earth. He had two horns like lamb but spoke like dragon. He made all inhabitants of earth worship the first beast. He forced everyone to have a mark on his right hand or forehead so that, no one could buy or sell unless the mark of the beast or the number of his name was on him.

Chapter 14 says that John looked up and saw a lamb stood on Mount Sion and with him a one lakh forty four thousand people having his father's name written on their foreheads. They sang a new song before the throne and before the four living creatures and twenty four elders. They are blameless.

John then saw three angels flying one after the other and singing. Then, he saw the harvest of the earth with sickle. He saw another sign in heaven, seven angels having the seven last plagues. One of the four living creatures gave to the seven angels, seven golden bowls filled with the wrath of God and heard a loud voice from the temple saying, "Go, pour out the seven bowls of God's wrath on the earth." When each angel poured out the bowls on earth one after the other, there were many plagues and earthquakes of very high intensity, when the great city split into three parts and all cities collapsed (Chapter 16).

Chapter 17 says that one of the seven angel came and told me "Come, I will show you the punishment of the great prostitute, who sits on many waters." I saw a woman sitting on a scarlet beast that was covered with blasphemous names and had seven heads and ten horns. It was written on her forehead "Mystery, Babylon the great, the mother of harlots and abominations of the earth."

Chapter 18 says, he saw another angel come down from heaven, having great power and the earth was lightened with his glory. The angel cried with a mighty voice, saying, "Babylon the great is fallen, is fallen, and is become the habitation of devils, and the hold of every foul spirit, and a cage of every unclean and hateful bird."

Chapter 19 says, he heard a great voice of many people in heaven, saying, "Alleluia, salvation and glory, and honour, and power, unto the Lord our God. The four beasts and twenty four elders fell down and worshipped God that sat on the throne, saying Amen, Alleluia."

Then, he saw a white horse with a rider on it. On his robe, it was written, "King of Kings and Lord of Lords."

Chapter 21 says, he saw a new heaven and a new earth, for the first heaven and first earth had passed away and there was no longer any sea. I saw the Holy City the New Jerusalem coming down out of heaven from God, prepared like a bride, beautifully dressed for her husband. Its brilliance was like that of a very precious jewel. It had a high wall with twelve gates and at the gates, twelve angels and the names of the twelve tribes of Israel written thereon. There were three gates on each side of the wall and the wall had twelve foundations and in them the names of the twelve apostles of the Lamb. But, there was no temple therein, for the Lord God Almighty and the Lamb are the temple in it. There was no need of the sun or moon to shine in it, for the glory of God did lighten it and the Lamb is the light thereof. There shall be no night there and nothing impure enters it.

In the final Chapter 22, it is said that the angel showed him the river of the water of life flowing from the throne of God and of the Lamb down the middle of the great street of the city. On each side of the river stood the trees of life, bearing twelve crops of fruit. The leaves of the tree are for the healing of the nations.

Then, the Lord said, "Behold, I am coming soon. Blessed is he who keeps the words of prophesy in this book. My reward is with me and I will give to every one according to what he has done. I am the Alpha and Omega, the first and the last, the beginning and the end. Blessed are those who wash their robes that they may have the right to the tree of life and may go through the gates into the city. I, Jesus have sent mine angel to testify unto you these things in the churches. I am the root and the offspring of David and the bright and morning star."

5.

Important Stories of the Old Testament and New Testament of the Holy Bible

In the Old Testament, as well as in the New Testament, there are very interesting stories, which every Christian child, particularly the Sunday School children should know from their young age. The mothers, as well as the Sunday School teachers and other elders will have to tell these stories to children, as they love to hear the stories. Grown up children will have to read these stories for themselves and if possible tell the younger children. By this, all the Christian children will come to know the interesting stories of the Bible from their young age and pass on their knowledge from generations to generations.

In order to enable the children, Sunday School teachers and mothers to choose any particular story quickly, the important stories of the Old Testament and New Testament have been briefly brought out in the following pages. These are arranged in the serial order and book-wise:-

5-A: IMPORTANT STORIES OF THE OLD TESTAMENT

BOOK NO.: 1- GENESIS

1. Creation of the world by God in the beginning (Chapter 1).

2. Story of the first man (Adam) and first woman (Eve) in the Garden of Eden (Chapter 2 and 3).

3. Story of two brothers, Cain and Abel – Sons of Adam and Eve (Chapter 4).

4. Story of Noah, the flood and the Ark (Chapter 5:28 to 32 and Chapters 6 to 9).

5. The Tower of Babel (Chapter 11:1 to 8).

6. Story of Abraham (Chapter 11:26 to 32, Chapters 12 to 25).

7. Story of Issac and Rebekah, their sons, Jacob and Esau (Chapter 24 and 25:19 to 34).

8. Story of Lot and his wife, who became a pillar of salt for disobeying God's command (Chapter 19).

9. Story of Joseph's younger days and as Chief in Egypt after he grew up (Chapter 37 to 50).

BOOK NO.: 2 – EXODUS

10. Birth of Moses, his adoption by Princess of Egypt and King Pharaoh's order to kill all the male children of Hebrew woman living in Egypt (Chapter 1 and 2).

11. Moses in Egypt, trying to liberate the Israelites (Chapter 4:18 to 31 and Chapters 5 and 6).

12. God's miracles in Egypt, like Aaron's staff becoming a snake, 10 plagues like 1) Water becoming blood, 2) Frogs, 3) Gnats, 4) Flies in entire country, 5) Death

of animals, 6) Boils on every ones body, 7) Hail storm, 8) Locusts in the country, 9) Darkness in the country, and 10) Death of the first born of all including son of King Pharaoh of Egypt (Chapters 7 to 12).

13. Israelites crossing the Red Sea with Moses ahead, as the water of Red Sea got separated (Chapter 13).

14. Israelites traveled for forty years from Egypt to Canaan through deserts and God provided food for them by raining "Manna" from heaven (Chapter 16).

15. When Israelites cried for drinking water in the desert, as commanded by God, Moses struck a rock at Horeb and drinking water came out of the rock. Moses called it as "Meribah" (Chapter 17).

16. Moses met the Lord on Mount Sinai and obtained Ten Commandments on two stone tablets (Chapter 20).

17. Moses stayed for forty days and forty nights on Mount Sinai, when the Lord instructed him how to make an "Ark of Covenant", Tabernacle, Table, Lamp Stand, Altar, Court Yard and all other items of worship (Chapter 25 to 30).

18. As Moses did not return from Mount Sinai for a long time, the Israelites asked Aaron to make a golden God resembling a calf and started worshipping it by singing and dancing before it. When Moses came down Mount Sinai with two tablets of Ten Commandments in his hands, he was furious to see all this and threw down the two tablets of Ten Commandments and broke them (Chapter 32).

19. As commanded by the Lord, Moses chiseled out two new stone tablets and took to the Lord on Mount Sinai and the Lord wrote with his hand once again, the Ten Commandments (Chapter 34).

20. Bezalel and Oholiab to whom the Lord had given the skills, started constructing the Ark, Tabernacle and all other items of worship (Chapters 36 to 40).

BOOK NO.: 3 – LEVITICUS

21. The Lord instructed Moses about all kinds of offerings, purification systems, various laws, etc. (Chapter 1 to 27).

BOOK NO.: 4 – NUMBERS

22. Moses sent twelve persons from the twelve tribes of Israelites to the promised land of Canaan to find out all about this new land. After forty days, they came back to Moses bringing with them bunches of grapes, figs and pomegranate fruits and said that Canaan was a country, where milk and honey flowed (Chapter 13).

23. Moses heard the murmurings of Israelites when they were on mount Nebo and God created fiery serpents and many died with serpent bite. They prayed to Moses to take away the serpents. As commanded by God, Moses made a big serpent with brass and kept it on mount Nebo, saying whoever was bitten by fiery serpent, if he looked at the brass serpent, he lived. It happened so (Chapter 21:4 to 9).

24. Balak, King of Moab was surrounded by Israelites – So, Balak requested King Balaam to help him. Balaam went riding on his donkey to help Balak to fight against Israelites. God did not like this. As Balaam was going on the donkey, on the way, the donkey saw an angel standing in the middle of the way to obstruct Balaam from going to help Balak. The donkey was terrified to see the angel and ran from the road into the fields. King Balaam was furious with the donkey and he had to beat it thrice. The donkey opened its mouth and told him of the vision of an angel. Balaam himself saw the

angel and fell on his face and worshipped God. As commanded by the Lord, Balaam changed the mind of Balak, as God was against him (Chapters 22 to 24).

BOOK NO.: 5 – DEUTERONOMY

25. Moses was forbidden by God to enter into the Promised Land (Jericho) by crossing River Jordan as he disobeyed the Lord by striking the rock at Meriba instead of only speaking to the rock as told by the Lord. Moses died on Mount Nebo in country of Jordan without crossing into Canaan (Chapter 3:21 to 29 and Chapter 34).

26. Before his death, Moses summoned all Israelites to him and read out the Ten Commandments and asked them to abondan idolatry and love the Lord (Chapters 5 to 13).

27. Moses recited a song before all Israelites, blessed all the tribes and died on Mount Nebo in the country of Jordan. Nobody knows his burial place till now. After Moses, Joshua took charge of the Israelites (Chapter 31 to 34).

BOOK NO.: 6 – JOSHUA

28. From here onwards, the attempts of Israelites to enter and conquer Canaan, the Promised Land, begins.

   Joshua made the priests (Levites) carry the Ark of the Covenant in front and lead all Israelite armies to cross river Jordan and capture the city of Jericho located on the banks of the river Jordan. As soon as the feet of the priests touched the waters of river Jordan, the water from up-stream stopped flowing and dry land was created for Israelite armies to cross the river Jordan (Chapter 3).

29. The fall of Jericho city to the Israelites armies is very interesting. The priests with the Ark on their shoulders

and the seven priests blowing their trumpets went round the city of Jericho once a day for six days and on the seventh day they went round seven times and when the trumpets sounded and all men of the Israelite armies shouted, the walls of Jericho city fell down. The Israelites armies entered the City of Jericho and killed everyone, except the family members of Rahab, who helped the Israelites spies earlier (Chapter 5:13 to 15 and Chapter 16).

30. The sun stood still day and night, when Joshua made his armies march whole night from Gilgal to Gibeon and defeated five kings of; 1) Jerusalem, 2) Hebron, 3) Jarmuth, 4) Lachish, and 5) Eglon, who were all killed (Chapter 10). In all, thirty one kings were defeated by the Israelite armies and their lands distributed amongst the tribes of Israelites.

31. Joshua was one hundred ten years old, when he called all leaders of Israelites and bid them farewell, blessed them, and died (Chapters 23 and 24).

BOOK NO.: 7 – JUDGES

32. Story of Deborah, the Prophetess (Chapter 4:4 to 24).

33. Story of Gideon, whom God chose under an oak tree to defeat Midianites and save Israelites (Chapter 6:11 to 22).

34. Story of mighty Samson and his wife, Delilah (Chapters 13 to 16).

BOOK NO.: 8 – RUTH

35. The story of Ruth and her mother-in-law, Naomi (Chapters 1 to 4).

BOOK NO.: 9 – I SAMUEL

36. Hannah, the wife of Elkanah had no children and was

constantly praying to God to bless her with a son, whom she would offer for God's service. When she was blessed with a son, she named him Samuel and offered him for the Lord's service by working along with Priest Eli in the temple (Chapters 1 and 2).

37. Samuel was sleeping in the temple along with Eli the priest, when the Lord called him thrice by his name. Samuel thought that it was the priest Eli calling him and went to him, but on the third time, Eli realized that it was the Lord calling Samuel (Chapter 3).

38. Israelites went out to fight against Philistines, but Israelites were defeated. The Ark of the Covenant was captured by the Philistines. The two sons of Eli also died. When the priest Eli heard about the capture of the Ark by the Philistines, he fell back and died. The Ark was taken by the Philistines and placed by the side of their God Dagon in Ashod. But, every morning the Philistines observed that their God Dagon had fallen on its face. So, they transferred the Ark to Gath and then to Ekron and finally returned to the Israelites. It was placed in the house of Abinadab, on the hill (Chapters 5 and 6).

39. Donkeys belonging to Kish, Father of Saul were missing. Saul went in search of them and met Samuel, who as commanded by the Lord, anointed Saul and made him the king (Chapters 9 and 10).

40. The Lord rejected Saul as the king and selected David the youngest son of Jesse of Bethlehem and anointed David, as a king (Chapters 15 and 16).

41. King Saul was troubled by an evil spirit and as advised by his men, he brought David to play the harp and relieve him, when the evil spirit tormented him. Saul liked David (Chapter 16:23).

42. The story of David and giant Goliath (Chapters 16 and 17).

When David was returning from battle, the women danced, singing, "Saul has slain thousands and David ten thousands." When King Saul heard this, he became jealous of David. Saul tried to kill David many times, but David escaped.

David and Jonathan, son of King Saul were very close friends from the beginning of David working with Saul in the palace (Chapters 18 to 20).

43. David escaped to deserts and caves of Adullam and Ein-Gedi on the eastern side of the country. But, King Saul chased David taking three thousand soldiers with him. In these caves, David spared King Saul twice without killing him, but just cutting the corner of his robe and taking away the spear and water jug of King Saul without the knowledge of all his three thousand soldiers, but did not kill him as he was the anointed King of God (Chapters 23, 24 and 26).

44. Philistines fought against Israelites on Mount Gilboa. They killed the three sons of King Saul and wounded King Saul critically. King Saul asked his armour bearer to kill him with his sword, but the armour bearer could not kill the king. So, King Saul fell on his own sword and died (Chapter 31).

BOOK NO.: 10 – II SAMUEL

45. David mourned for many days over the death of his bosom friend Jonathan, son of King Saul. David was made the King of Judah first and later on King of entire Israel, when he was just thirty years old (Chapter 2:1 to 7 and Chapter 5:1 to 5).

46. The Ark of the Covenant was brought by King David from the house of Abinadab to the city of David (Mount Sion), keeping it for some days in the house of Obed Edom. As the Ark was entering the city of David, he danced before it. David's wife, Michal, the daughter

of King Saul, saw David dancing and did not like David being a king dancing like an ordinary man before the Ark (Chapter 6).

47. Absalom, son of King David had a sad death, as the mule he was riding went under the thick branches of a large oak tree and his long hair was caught in the branches, but the mule ran away, making Absalom hang in the air. Then, Joab commander of David's army took three javelins and plunged them into the heart of Absalom, who was hanging. Absalom died. King David heard of this and cried bitterly, saying "O my son, Absalom, O Absalom, my son, my son (Chapter 18).

48. David sang a song of praise, as the Lord delivered him from the hands of all his enemies (Chapter 22).

BOOK NO.: 11 – I KINGS

49. King David made his son, Solomon as the king (Chapter 1:28 to 52).

50. King Solomon had a dream, when he was in Gibeon. The Lord said to Solomon in the dream, "Ask, what ever you want me to give you." King Solomon asked the Lord to give him the wisdom only to judge right and wrong. Lord gave him wisdom.

One day, two women in his kingdom fought for one baby, each claiming the baby as hers. King Solomon due to his wisdom correctly judged and determined the real mother of the baby and handed over the baby to her (Chapter 3:16 to 28).

51. Queen Sheba heard about King Solomon's wisdom and came to King Solomon to test him by asking many clever questions. King Solomon answered all her questions without any difficulty. Queen Sheba was surprised and was convinced that King Solomon was really a wise king. While coming, Queen Sheba brought

many expensive gifts to King Solomon, who also gave her many gifts while going away (Chapter 4:29 to 34 and Chapter 10).

52. King Solomon successfully completed the construction of a magnificent temple for the Lord in Jerusalem and dedicated it with very long prayers (Chapters 5 to 8).

53. Prophet Elijah was fed by the ravens as ordered by the Lord. He blessed the jar of flour and the jug of oil belonging to the widow not to diminish. Later on, when the son of the widow died, Elijah raised him up (Chapter 17).

54. Prophet Elijah proved on Mount Carmel in the presence of four hundred and fifty prophets of their God Baal and four hundred prophets of their God Asherah that the Lord was the real God, as he consumed the burnt offering of Elijah and not the offerings of the other prophets. Prophet Elijah killed all these prophets with his sword (Chapter 18:16 to 40).

55. Elisha, who was ploughing his fields was blessed by Prophet Elijah and Elisha left everything and followed Prophet Elijah (Chapter 19:19 to 21).

BOOK NO.: 12 – II KINGS

56. Prophets Elijah and Elisha went to the river Jordan. Elijah struck the waters of the river with his cloak and the water was separated. Both of them crossed the river on dry land and as they were walking, suddenly a chariot of fire and horses of fire appeared and separated Elijah and Elisha. Elijah went up to heaven in a whirlwind. Elisha saw this and cried, saying, "O my Father, my Father." Then Elisha took the cloak of Elijah that had fallen down when Elijah was being taken up to heaven and Elisha struck the waters of river Jordan, when they got separated leaving a dry land for Elisha to cross.

Elisha went to the nearby city of Jericho (Chapter 2).

57. The people of Jericho came to Elisha and told him that the water in Jericho was unproductive. Elisha sprinkled salt on the water and it became productive. This is now known as "Elisha Spring" till today in Jericho (Chapter 2:19 to 22).

58. Prophet Elisha performed many miracles, like multiplying oil in the house of a poor widow, raising the dead son of a Shunammite woman, feeding one hundred men with twenty loaves, healing the army commander by name Naaman of his leprosy, making an iron axe that had fallen into water to float and many more miracles (Chapters 4 to 6).

59. King Nebuchadnezzar of Babylon raided Jerusalem, destroyed the walls of Jerusalem, burnt the temple and carried away all the gold, silver and precious articles of the temple to Babylon. He also took King Zedekiah as prisoner to Babylon (Chapter 24 and 25).

BOOK NOS.: 13 & 14: I & II CHRONICLES

60. These two chronicles deal with the stories of King David, and King Solomon explained earlier in I Samuel and II Samuel, I Kings and II Kings. So, these are repetition. Hence, they are not explained here once again.

BOOK NO.: 15 – EZRA

61. King Cyrus of Persia started rebuilding of the destroyed temple in Jerusalem and many Israelites, who were taken to Babylon as prisoners and as slaves started returning to Jerusalem and helped Cyrus in completing the temple with all pomp and show (Chapters 1 and 2).

62. Ezra, the priest and teacher also returned from Babylon to Jerusalem along with the Israelites (Chapters 7 and 8).

BOOK NO.: 16 – NEHEMIAH

63. Nehemiah also came to Jerusalem and reconstructed the broken walls of Jerusalem city and dedicated them (Chapter 2 and 3).

BOOK NO.: 17 – ESTHER

64. Esther was an ordinary Jewish girl staying with her uncle in Persia. The king wanted to marry a beautiful girl after he dethroned his first wife. Esther was shown to the king and he liked her and married her. Esther made all efforts to save the Israelites from the cruel hands of the Persian officers and she ultimately saved them all (Chapters 1 to 10).

BOOK NO.: 18 – JOB

No interesting stories in this book.

BOOK NO.: 19 – PSALMS

No interesting stories in this book. All these are psalms of King David.

BOOK NO.: 20 – PROVERBS

No interesting stories in this book. These are proverbs of King Solomon.

BOOK NO.: 21 – ECCLESIASTES

No interesting stories in this book.

BOOK NO.: 22 – SONG OF SONGS

No interesting stories in this book. These are songs of King Solomon.

BOOK NO.: 23 – ISAIAH

No interesting stories in this book.

BOOK NO.: 24 – JEREMIAH

No interesting stories in this book.

BOOK NO.: 25 – LAMENTATIONS

No interesting stories in this book.

BOOK NO.: 26 – EZEKIEL

No interesting stories in this book.

BOOK NO.: 27 – DANIEL

65. This book contains the interesting story of Daniel (Belteshazzar), Shadrach (Hananiah), Meshach (Mishael) and Abednego (Azariah). The names in brackets were given to them in Babylon. Daniel was noted for interpreting dreams, particularly dreams of King Nebuchadnazzer of Babylon (Chapters 1 and 2).

66. The story of Shadrach, Meshach and Abednego, who were thrown into a furnace, as they did not bow before the huge image of gold made by King Nebuchadnazzer, but God saved them miraculously and even their hair was not burnt. This made the king accept the God of these three men as true God and made everyone in his country to accept it (Chapter 3).

67. King Nebuchadnazzer's dream of a tree very huge in its height, branches, etc. but a voice from heaven made it to be cut. Another dream of writing on a wall were correctly interpreted by Daniel, but all the experts in the kingdom of Nebuchadnazzer could not interpret (Chapter 4 and 5).

68. The next king of Babylon by name Darius ordered that Daniel, who was praying to his own God and not the king, should be thrown into the den of lions. It was done, and the king could not sleep, whole night. Next day, early in the morning, the king went to the den of lions and was stunned to observe that the lions had not harmed Daniel (Chapter 6).

69. Daniel's dreams of, 1) Four beasts, 2) A ram and a goat, 3) Vision of a man, etc. (Chapters 7 to 10).

BOOK NO.: 28 – HOSEA

No interesting stories in this book.

BOOK NO.: 29 – JOEL

No interesting stories in this book.

BOOK NO.: 30 – AMOS

No interesting stories in this book.

BOOK NO.: 31 – OBADIAH

No interesting stories in this book.

BOOK NO.: 32 – JONAH

70. This book deals with the interesting story of Jonah. God asked Jonah to go to the city of Nineveh and advise the people there to refrain from sin. But, Jonah did not like to go to Nineveh. So, he went to the port of Joppa and got into a ship, which was going to Tarshih. A violent storm broke on the sea and all in the ship had to cast lots as to who was responsible for this storm. The lot fell on Jonah. They all pushed him into the sea and the storm stopped. God made a big fish swallow Jonah and he was in the belly of the fish for three days

and prayed to God, who made the fish vomit Jonah on a dry land (Chapters 1 and 2).

BOOK NO.: 33 – MICAH

No interesting stories in this book.

BOOK NO.: 34 – NAHUM

71. The fall of the city of Nineveh is explained in this book (Chapters 1 and 2).

BOOK NO.: 35 – HABAKKUK

No interesting stories in this book.

BOOK NO.: 36 – ZEPHANIAH

No interesting stories in this book.

BOOK NO.: 37 – HAGGAI

No interesting stories in this book.

BOOK NO.: 38 – ZECHARIAH

72. Prophet Zechariah had a vision of; 1) A man among the Myrtle trees riding on a red horse, 2) Four horns and four craftsmen, 3) A man with measuring a line in his hand, 4) Clean garments for High Priests, 5) Gold Lamp stand and two olive trees, 6) Flying Scroll, 7) A woman in a basket, and 8) Four chariots (Chapters 1 to 6).

BOOK NO.: 39 – MALACHI

No interesting stories in this book.

5-B: IMPORTANT STORIES OF THE NEW TESTAMENT

BOOK NO.: 1 – MATTHEW

1. Jesus belongs to forty second generation of Abraham. There were fourteen generations from Abraham to David, fourteen generations from David to the exile of Israelites to Babylon and fourteen generations from exile up to Jesus (Chapter 1:1 to 17).

2. Birth of Jesus in Bethlehem, fleeing of Joseph with Mary and Baby Jesus to Egypt to escape killing by the orders of King Herod and return to Nazareth after King Herod died (Chapter 2).

3. Baptism of Jesus by John the Baptist in river Jordan (Chapter 3:1 to 17).

4. Temptation of Jesus, who fasted for forty days and forty nights (Chapter 4:1 to 11).

5. Jesus called his first disciples (Simon Peter, and his brother Andrew, James and his brother John) who were all fishermen in the Sea of Galilee (Chapter 4:18 to 22).

6. Sermon on the mountain – Jesus preached to the multitudes from a mountain, telling them of the eight blessings (eight beatitudes) (Chapter 5:1 to 12).

7. Jesus performed many miracle like 1) healing a man having leprosy, 2) healing a servant of a centurian in Capernaum, 3) healing the mother in law of Peter, as she had high fever, 4) Arresting the storm on the sea of Galilee on which his disciples were going in a boat, 5) Healing 2 men possessed by demons, 6) Healing a paralytic, 7) Raising a dead girl, 8) Healing a women, who was sick for twelve years, 9) Healing the blind and mute and many more (Chapters 8 and 9).

   All the miracles are explained in a separate chapter at the end of this book.

8. Jesus narrated many parables to make people understand the heavenly things easily, some of which are – 1) Parable of a sower, 2) Parable of the weeds among the wheat, 3) Parable of mustard seed, 4) Parable of yeast, 5) Parable of hidden treasure and the pearl, 6) Parable of a net and many more parables. Jesus explained some of them to his disciples also privately. All these parables are explained separately in a chapter at the end of this book.

9. Jesus walked on the waters of the Sea of Galilee (Chapter 14:22-36).

10. Jesus fed five thousand men with five loaves and two fishes and twelve baskets full of remnants were collected (Chapter 14:13-21).

11. Again, Jesus fed four thousand men with seven loaves and a few small fishes and seven baskets full of remnants were collected (Chapter 15:29 to 39).

12. Transfiguration of Jesus on a mountain (Chapter 17:1 to 11).

13. Jesus loves little children (Chapter 19:13 to 15).

14. Parable of workers in a vineyard (Chapter 20:1 to16).

15. Jesus entered Jerusalem sitting on a donkey and people that followed were singing "Hosanna" (Chapter 21:1 to 11).

16. Jesus drove out all sellers of goods from the Jerusalem temple (Chapter 21: 12 to 17).

17. Jesus cursed a fig tree in Bethany and it dried (Chapter 21:18 to 22).

18. Jesus narrated parables of the two sons, parable of tenants, parable of wedding banquet (Chapter 21:28 to 46 and 22:1 to 14).

19. Jesus narrated parable of ten virgins, parable of talents (Chapter 25:1 to 30).

20. Last supper of Jesus with his disciples in the Upper Room. Jesus prayed in the Garden of Gethsemane on Mount of Olives and Jesus was arrested (Chapter 26:17 to 56).

21. Jesus was taken to Caiaphas the chief priest, then to Pontius Pilot and Herod and was condemned to death by crucifiction (Chapter 26:57 to 75 and 1 to 26).

22. Jesus was crucified on Calvary and after he died on the cross, his body was placed in the rock tomb of Joseph Arimathia in a garden(Chapter 27:32 to 65).

23. On the third day, Jesus rose from the dead and appeared to Mary Magdalene, and later on, to his disciples (Chapter 28).

BOOK NO.: 2 – MARK

24. Mission of John the Baptist and Baptism of Jesus in river Jordan by John the Baptist (Chapter 1:1 to 8).

25. Jesus fasted for forty days and his temptation (Chapter 1:9 to 13).

26. Jesus selected his first four disciples (Chapter 1:14 to 20).

27. Jesus narrated many parables, like 1) Parable of the sower, 2) Parable of the growing seed, 3) Parable of the mustard seed, etc. (Chapter 4:1 to 34).

28. Jesus arrested the storm on the Sea of Galilee (Chapter 4:35 to 41).

29. Jesus healed many sick people, like 1) A man possessed by a demon, 2) Raised Jairus's daughter, who was dead, 3) Healed a woman having a disease for twelve years, and many more (Chapter 5:1 to 43).

30. Jesus fed five thousand men with five loaves and two fishes and twelve baskets full of remnants were collected (Chapter 6:30 to 44).

31. Jesus walked on the waters of the Sea of Galilee (Chapter 6:30 to 44).

32. Again, Jesus fed four thousand men with seven loaves and a few small fishes and seven baskets full of remnants were collected (Chapter 8:1 to 9).

33. Jesus was transfigured on a mountain (Chapter 9:1 to 13).

34. Jesus loves little children (Chapter 10:13 to 16).

35. Jesus entered Jerusalem sitting on a donkey and the people who followed him sang "Hosanna" (Chapter 11:1 to 11).

36. Jesus entered the temple and drove away all the sellers of goods and moneychangers (Chapter 11:12 to 19).

37. Jesus cursed a fig tree and it dried up (Chapter 12 to 14 and 20 to 25).

38. Jesus said that the offering of a poor widow was more than others (Chapter 12:41 to 43).

39. Jesus was anointed by a woman in Bethany (Chapter 14:1 to 11).

40. Jesus had his last supper with his twelve disciples in the Upper Room and went to the Garden of Gethsemane on Mount of Olives to pray and was arrested there (Chapter 14:12 to 51).

41. Jesus was taken to the High Priest, later to Pontius Pilot for judgement. Peter denied Jesus thrice before the cock crew. Jesus was condemned to death by crucifixion (Chapter 14:53 to 72 and Chapter 15:1 to 20).

42. Jesus was crucified at Golgotha (Place of skull) on mount Calvary and when he died on the cross, his body was placed in the rock tomb of Joseph of Arimathia (Chapter 15:21 to 47).

43. On the third day, Jesus rose from the dead and after appearing to his disciples, he ascended to heaven at Bethany, after blessing his disciples (Chapter 16).

BOOK NO.: 3 – LUKE

44. Birth of John the Baptist (Chapter 1:5 to 25 and 57 to 80).

45. Birth of Jesus in Bethlehem (Chapter 1:26 to 56 and 2:1 to 51).

46. Jesus fasted for forty days and was tempted by satan (Chapter 4:1 to 13).

47. Jesus selected his first four disciples on the shores of Sea of Galilee (Chapter 5:1 to 11).

48. Jesus performed miracles like, 1) Drove out an evil spirit from a man, 2) Healed a man having leprosy, 3) Healed a paralytic man, etc. (Chapter 4:31 to 41 and 5:1 to 25).

49. Jesus narrated many parables like, 1) A sower, 2) Lamp on a stand, 3) Parable of a Good Samaritan, 4) Parable of a rich man, 5) Parable of a mustard seed, 6) Parable of yeast, 7) Parable of a great banquet, 8) Parable of the lost sheep, 9) Parable of a lost coin, 10) Parable of a lost son, 11) Parable of a manager of a rich man, 12) Parable of a persistent widow, 13) Parable of the pharisee and a tax collector, and 14) Parable of ten minas, etc. (Chapters 8:1 to 15, 8:16 to 18, Chapter 10:25 to 37, Chapter 12:13 to 21, Chapter 13:18 to 26, Chapter 14:15 to 24, Chapter 15:1 to 32, Chapter 16:1 to 12, Chapter 18:1 to 10 and Chapter 14:11 to 26).

50. Jesus stopped the storm on the Sea of Galilee (Chapter 8:22 to 25).

51. Jesus healed many sick people like, 1) A man possessed by demon, 2) Raised the daughter of Jairus as she was dead, 3) Healed a woman who was sick for twelve years, 4) Healed a boy possessed by evil spirit, 5) Healed a crippled woman, etc. (Chapter 5:12 to 25,

Chapter 7:1 to 17, Chapter 8:26 to 56, Chapter 9:37 to 45, Chapter 13:10 to 17, Chapter 17:11 to 17).

52. Jesus loves little children (Chapter 18:15 to 17).

53. Jesus went to Jericho and saw Zachhaeus, who climbed up a sycamore tree to see Jesus passing by and Jesus went to his house and dined with him (Chapter 19:1 to 9).

54. Jesus entered Jerusalem, sitting on a donkey and the people who followed him sang "Hosanna" (Chapter 19:28 to 44).

55. Jesus entered the Jerusalem temple and drove out the moneychangers and all selling goods (Chapter 19:45 to 48).

56. Jesus had his last supper with his disciples in the Upper Room and went to the Garden of Gethsemane on the Mount of Olives to pray and was arrested (Chapter 22:1 to 53).

57. Peter denied Jesus thrice before the cock crew (Chapter 22:54 to 62).

58. Jesus was judged by Pontius Pilot and was condemned to death by crucifixion (Chapter 22:66 to 71 and 23:1 to 25).

59. Jesus was crucified, he spoke seven words from the cross and died on the cross (Chapter 23:26 to 55).

60. Jesus rose from the dead on the third day, appeared to his disciples, and ascended to heaven (Chapter 24).

BOOK NO.: 4 – JOHN

61. Jesus selected his first four disciples (Chapter 1:35 to 51).

62. Jesus performed his first miracle of changing water into wine at a wedding in Cana (Chapter 2:1 to 11).

63. Jesus drove away those that were selling sheep and doves from the temple, saying, "How dare you turn my Father's house into a market! Get out from here (Chapter 2:13 to 16).

64. Jesus met a Samaritan woman at Jacob's well in Sycar and told her past (Chapter 4:1 to 26).

65. Jesus healed a sick person at the pool of Bethesda, as he was waiting there for many years (Chapter 5:1 to 14).

66. Jesus fed five thousand men with five loaves and two fishes. His disciples collected twelve baskets full of remnants (Chapter 6:1 to 14).

67. Jesus walked on the water of the Sea of Galilee (Chapter 6:16 to 24).

68. Jesus raised Lazarus, who was dead (Chapter 11:1 to 44).

69. Jesus was anointed in Bethany (Chapter 12:1 to 10).

70. Jesus entered Jerusalem sitting on a donkey and the people following him were singing "Hosanna" (Chapter 12:12 to 19).

71. Jesus washed the feet of his disciples. He said that Peter would deny him thrice before the cock crew (Chapter 13:1 to 38).

72. Jesus went with his disciples to the Garden of Gethsemane on Mount of Olives to pray. He was arrested and taken to Caiaphas and High Priest and then to Pontius Pilot for judgement and he was condemned to death by crucifixion (Chapter 18 and 19:1 to 16).

73. Jesus carried a heavy cross on his shoulders from "Gabbatha" (Judgement Hall) to "Golgotha" (Place of Skull) where he was nailed to the cross (Crucified). After Jesus died on the cross, his body was placed in the rock tomb of Joseph of Arimathia (Chapter 19:17 to 42).

74. After three days, Jesus rose from the dead and appeared to his disciples. Last time, he appeared to his disciples who were fishing in the Sea of Galilee (Tibereas) and made them catch one hundred fifty three big fishes. Jesus ate with them and asked Peter, "Feed my Lambs, Take care of my sheep" (Chapter 21:1 to 15).

BOOK NO.: 5 – ACTS

75. Believer, Stephen was stoned to death (Chapter 7:54 to 60).

76. Saul, who was persecuting Christians saw a vision on his way to Damascus and became blind. He was led by his followers by hand to Damascus, where Ananias, as commanded by the Lord prayed and opened his eyes. Saul was converted as a Christian and began to preach about Jesus (Chapter 9:1 to 31).

77. Peter had a vision on the rooftop, when he saw all kinds of beasts coming down from heaven on a big sheet (Chapter 10:9 to 21).

BOOK NO.: 6 – ROMANS

No interesting stories in this book.

BOOK NO.: 7 – I CORINTHIANS

No interesting stories in this book.

BOOK NO.: 8 – II CORINTHIANS

No interesting stories in this book.

BOOK NO.: 9 – GALATIANS

No interesting stories in this book.

BOOK NO.: 10 – EPHESIANS

78. Saul, now known as Paul advised wives, husbands, children, parents, slaves and masters (Chapters 5 and 6).

BOOK NO.: 11 – PHILIPPIANS

No interesting stories in this book.

BOOK NO.: 12 – COLOSSIANS

79. Paul advised wives, husbands, children, parents, fathers, slaves and masters (Chapter 3:18 to 25).

BOOK NO.: 13 – I THESSALONIANS

No interesting stories in this book.

BOOK NO.: 14 – II THESSALONIANS

No interesting stories in this book.

BOOK NO.: 15 – I TIMOTHY

80. Paul advised widows, elders, slaves (Chapter 5).

BOOK NO.: 16 – II TIMOTHY

No interesting stories in this book.

BOOK NO.: 17 – TITUS

No interesting stories in this book.

BOOK NO.: 18 – PHILEMON

No interesting stories in this book.

BOOK NO.: 19 – HEBREWS

No interesting stories in this book.

BOOK NO.: 20 – JAMES

No interesting stories in this book.

BOOK NO.: 21 – I PETER

81. Peter advised wives and husbands (Chapter 3:1 to 7).

BOOK NO.: 22 – II PETER

No interesting stories in this book.

BOOK NO.: 23 – I JOHN

Peter advised the children and said, love one another (Chapter 2:28 to 30 and Chapter 3:1 to 24).

BOOK NO.: 24 – II JOHN

No interesting stories in this book.

BOOK NO.: 25 – III JOHN

No interesting stories in this book.

BOOK NO.: 26 – JUDE

No interesting stories in this book.

BOOK NO.: 27 – REVELATION

82. Different visions Apostle John saw are explained in all the chapters of this book.

6.

Parables in the Old Testament, in Serial Order

1. Abimelech, the son of Jerubbaal went to Shechem, collected money from his mother's relatives and killed three score and ten sons of Jerubbaal and his father. But, Jotham, the youngest son escaped, as he hid himself. Abimelech was made the king by all men of Shechem.

   When they told Jotham all this, he stood on the top of Mount Gerizim and told everyone, the parable of trees proposing olive tree, fig tree and vine to be their king, but all refused. Then, they finally asked Bramble bush to reign over them. Bramble bush said, if you want me to be your king, then come and put your trust in my shadow; if not, let fire come out of bramble and devour. Jotham said that if you have made Abimelech, son of a maidservant and who had killed three score and ten children of Jerubbaal, my father as your king, rejoice in him and let him also rejoice in you (Judges 9:1 to 21).

2. Samson was a very strong man. When he was going to a place, Timnath to see a Philistine girl, a young lion pounced on him. Samson killed it with his bare hands. After a few days, when he saw the carcass of the lion,

he saw honeybees and honey in the carcass. Samson took the honey and he gave it to his parents also, but he did not tell from where he got the honey.

After Samson returned home, he told his thirty companions a riddle to be solved by them in seven days, failing which thirty sheets and thirty changes of garments were to be given to losers or winners. The riddle was, "Out of the eater came forth meat and out of the strong came forth sweetness." None of his companions could solve this riddle. Samson's wife wept for seven days, asking Samson to tell her the answer. At last, Samson pitied her on the seventh day and told her the answer, which she revealed to the thirty men. On the seventh day, they solved this riddle before Samson, saying, "What is sweeter than honey and what is stronger than lion?" (Judges 14:5 to 20).

3. King David took the wife of his commander, Uriah as his wife after arranging her husband to be killed in a battle. God was displeased with this act of King David. Lord sent Prophet Nathan to David to tell him a parable. Nathan said, "There were two men in a city, one was rich and the other was poor. The rich man had many lambs but the poor man had only one lamb, which was like his own daughter, eating and drinking with his children and sleeping with him. One day, the rich man had a guest and in order to feed him, the rich man did not kill any lamb out of his many lambs, to dress for the traveller guest, but the rich man took the poor man's only pet lamb and dressed it (prepared the meal) for his guest."

On hearing this, King David was furious with the rich man and said to Prophet Nathan that this rich man should be killed and four lambs should be given to the poor man.

Then, Prophet Nathan told King David that, "You are that rich man. The Lord God of Israel said that he anointed you as King of Israel and gave you everything but you have done evil in His sight. You have killed Uriah and took his wife as your wife and God will punish you suitably." King David realized his evil (II Samuel 12:1to 13).

4. Joab perceived that King David's heart was towards his son, Absalom, who fled to Geshur. Joab fetched a wise woman from Tekoah and taught how to speak before the King David. She fell before the king crying and said, "I am a widow and I had two sons. They fought among themselves and one killed the other. Now, the whole family wants to kill the living son." King David said, "So long as I live, not one hair of thy son will fall to the earth." The woman said, "The king doth speak this thing as one which is faulty, in that the king doth not fetch home again his banished."

    King David realized that these words were taught to her by Joab. King David sent Joab to bring Absalom and after sometime, King David kissed Absalom.

    (II Samuel 14:1 to 33).

5. Benhadad was brought to his brother King Ahab, who made a covenant with him and sent him away.

    A certain man of the sons of Prophets said unto his neighbour in the word of the Lord, "Smite me, I pray thee." And the man refused to smite him. Then, said he unto him, "Because, thou hast not obeyed the voice of the Lord, behold! as soon as thou art departed from me, a lion shall slay thee." And as soon as he was departed from him, a lion found him, and slew him. Then he found another man and said, "Smite me, I pray thee." And the man smote him, so that in smiting, he wounded him.

    So, the Prophet departed, and waited for the king by the way, and disguised himself with ashes upon his face. And as the king passed by, he cried unto the King and said, "Thy servant went out into the midst of the battle: and behold! a man turned aside and brought a man unto me, and said, keep this man: if by any means he be missing, then shall thy life be for his life, or else thou shalt pay a talent of silver."

And as thy servant was busy here and there, he was gone. The king of Israel said to him. So, shall thy judgement be; thyself hast decided it. And he hasted and took the ashes away from his face; and the King of Israel discerned him that he was of the prophets. And he said unto the King, "Thus saith the Lord, because thou hast let go out of thy hand a man whom I appointed to utter destruction, therefore thy life shall go for his life, and thy people for his people. And the King of Israel went to his house heavy and displeased, and came to Samaria " (I Kings 20:33 to 43).

6. King Ahab called the Prophet Micaiah and asked him whether he should go against Ramoth gilead to battle, or shall he forbear. Micaiah answered, "Go and prosper; for the Lord shall deliver it into the hands of the King." Micaiah further said, "I saw the Lord sitting on his throne, and all the hosts of heaven standing by him on his right hand and on his left. And the Lord said, "Who shall persuade Ahab, that he may go up and fall at Ramoth-gilead?" And one said on this manner, and another said on that manner. And, therefore, came forth a spirit and stood before the Lord, and said, "I will persuade him." And the Lord said unto him, "Wherewith?" and he said, "I will go forth and I will be a lying spirit in the mouth of the prophets." And he said, "Thou shalt persuade him and prevail also: go forth and do so."

Now, therefore, behold, the Lord hath put a lying spirit in the mouth of all these thy prophets, and the Lord hath spoken evil concerning thee.
(I Kings 22:13 to 23).

7. Then, Amaziah sent messengers to Jehoash, the son of Jehoahaz son of Jehu, King of Israel saying, come, let us look one another in the face.

    And Jehoash, the King of Israel sent to Amaziah King of Judah saying, "The thistle that was in Lebanon, sent to the cedar in Lebanon saying, Give thy daughter to my son to wife : and there passed by a wild beast that was in Lebanon and trode down the thistle (II Kings 14:9)

8. A heavy drinker of wine, which in the end bites like a snake and poisons like a viper and Israelites are like drunkards (Proverbs 23:29 to 35).

9. The people of Israel are like the field of the sluggard with thorns and weeds every-where and wall in ruins (Proverbs 24:30 to 34).

10. The people of Israel are like a vineyard well taken care of, but yielded bad fruit (Isaiah 5:1 to 6).

11. Israel is like a farmer who knows how to plough and sow different seeds, as this comes from the Lord (Isaiah 28:23 to 29).

12. Two great eagles and vine plant (Ezekiel 17:1 to 10).

13. A lioness brought up her cubs and they were caught in a pit and another in a net and sent to Egypt and Babylon and out in prison and their roar was not heard on the mountains of Israel (Ezekiel 19:1 to 9).

14. Two adulterous sisters compared to the people of Israel (Ezekiel 23).

15. The cooking pot with bones boiling in it, compared to the people of Israel (Ezekiel 24: 3 to 5).

16. Cedar tree of Lebanon, with very great height and wide branches resulting in other trees envying it. Lord handed it over to the rulers of Nations (Ezekiel 31: 1 to 11).

17. King Pharaoh of Egypt is like a monster in the sea, but the Lord will throw it on land to be eaten by all birds and the sword of the king of Babylon will come against Egypt (Ezekial 32:1 to 16).

18. The Lord said that the shepherds do not take care of the sheep and without a shepherd the sheep are scattered and eaten by wild animals. The shepherds are accountable for the flock (Ezekiel 34).

19. The Lord showed a valley full of dried bones. On prophesy as the Lord commanded, the dried bones came together, flesh grew on them and they breathed and stood on their legs (Ezekiel 37).

20. The living water of a river (Ezekiel 47).

7.

Miracles in the Old Testament, in Serial Order

1. Destruction of the cities of Sodom and Gomorrah – The sin of people of Sodom and Gomorrah were so grievous that the Lord rained down burning sulfur and burnt all people, and vegetation (Genesis 19:24).

2. Lot's wife turned into a salt pillar as she looked back at Sodom (Genesis 19:26).

3. Birth of Issac-Sarah was blessed by Lord to give birth to Issac, when she and Abraham were very old (Genesis 21:2).

4. Burning bush, but not destroyed - Moses was tending the flock of sheep near Mount Horeb, when he saw an angel appeared to him in flames of fire from within a bush but the bush did not burn up (Exodus 3:2).

5. Aaron's rod changed into a serpent - Moses and Aaron went to King Pharaoh and as the Lord commanded, Aaron threw his staff before Pharaoh and it became a snake (Exodus 7:8 to 10).

6. The Lord brought ten plagues into Egypt so that King Pharaoh could let the Israelites go out of Egypt: Water

turned into blood - As commanded by the Lord, Moses and Aaron struck the waters of river Nile and its water was changed into blood. All the water in Egypt was turned into blood and there was no drinking water (Exodus 7:14 to 24).

7. Frogs throughout Egypt – As Lord commanded, Aaron stretched out his hand over the waters in Egypt and frogs came out and covered the land (Exodus 8:6 to 8)

8. Gnats throughout Egypt – As the Lord commanded, Aaron stretched out his staff and struck the dust of the land and it turned into gnats and came upon men and animals (Exodus 8:16 to 18).

9. The plague of flies in Egypt – As the Lord commanded, Moses said to King Pharaoh that if he did not allow Israelites to go out of Egypt, there would be swarms of flies throughout Egypt, except the land of Goshen, where Israelites stayed. So, the flies destroyed the entire land of Egypt (Exodus 8:20 to 24).

10. Plague on livestock – All animals like horses, donkey, sheep, and goats in Egypt died, but not one animal belonging to Israelites died (Exodus 9:1 to 7).

11. Plague of boils on the body – As commanded by the Lord, Moses took soot from a furnace and tossed it into the air before the Pharaoh and every person and animals got festering boils on their bodies (Exodus 9:8 to 10).

12. Hailstorm over Egypt – As the Lord commanded, Moses stretched out his staff towards the sky and the Lord sent thunder and hail and lightening flashed down to the ground by which all crops and trees were destroyed (Exodus 9:23 to 25).

13. Plague of Locusts – As Lord commanded, Moses stretched out his hand over Egypt and swarms of locusts came over entire Egypt and destroyed the fields etc. (Exodus 10:12 to 20).

14. Plague of darkness over Egypt – As the Lord commanded, Moses stretched out his hand and darkness covered the entire Egypt for three days and not in the place where Israelites lived (Exodus 10:21 to 23).

15. The death of the first born – Moses summoned all the elders of Israel and told them to slaughter the passover lamb and put the blood on the top and on both sides of the door frames. When the Lord went through the land to strike down the first born of everyone, he saw the sign of blood on doors of Israelites, and did not strike the first born, but the Lord struck all the first born of Egyptians and there was loud wailing in Egypt. Then, King Pharaoh allowed the Egyptians to leave Egypt (Exodus 12:21 to 36).

16. Red Sea water got separated – As Israelites were leaving Egypt with the permission of King Pharaoh of Egypt, they had to cross the Red Sea. Moses stretched out his hand over the sea. The water got separated, leaving a dry land for Israelites to cross the sea. The water remained as walls to their right and left till they all crossed the sea (Exodus 14:19 to 23).

17. The bitter water of Marah was turned as sweet drinking water – When the Israelites traveled for three days from the Red Sea in the desert, there was no drinking water, as the water at Marah in shur desert was bitter. When they appealed to Moses, he prayed and God asked Moses to throw a piece of wood into the water and it was turned as sweet drinking water (Exodus 15:22 to 27).

18. Lord rained Manna (food) in the morning and Quail (meat) in the evenings for the Israelites in the desert – As the Israelites travelled for two and half months from Egypt, they came to the desert of Sin, between Elim and Sinai. Israelites grumbled against Moses and Aaron as there was no food like in Egypt. But the Lord said,

"I will rain down bread from heaven and they have to collect it in six days and on the seventh day (Sabbath) there will be no bread from heaven and on the sixth day itself they have to collect for seventh day of Sabbath. The Israelites called this bread from heaven "Manna" (Exodus 16:1 to 34).

19. Drinking water from a rock at Rephidim – As the Israelites travelled from the desert of sin till Rephidim, they quarreled with Moses for drinking water. But, as Lord commanded, Moses struck a rock with his staff and water came out of the rock. This place is called "Massah" or "Meribah" (Exodus 17:1 to 7).

20. Nadab and Abihu, sons of Aaron were consumed by heavenly fire – Nadab and Abihu, sons of Aaron took their censers, put fire in them, and added incense and they offered unauthorized fire before Lord, contrary to his command. So, fire came out from the Lord and consumed them, and they died (Leviticus 10:1 to 3).

21. Fire from the Lord burnt outskirts of the camp – Israelites complained about their hardships to Moses and the Lord was angry. Then, fire from the Lord burned and consumed some of the outskirts of the camp. This place is called "Taberah", because fire from the Lord burned the camp (Numbers 11:1 to 3).

22. Korah, son of Izhar was swallowed by the earth and two hundred fifty followers of Korah were consumed by heavenly fire – Korah and two other persons rose up against Moses and they had two hundred fifty followers, who wanted to be leaders. Lord punished them all as the earth opened up and swallowed Korah and all his families, and fire came down from heaven and consumed all the two hundred fifty men (Numbers 16:1 to 35).

23. Aaron's staff – out of all the staffs of twelve tribes Aaron's staff budded and blossomed and produced

almonds – Lord said to Moses to collect twelve staff of the twelve tribes of all Israelites with their names written on each and on the staff of Levi, write Aaron's name and place them in the Tent of meeting and the staff belonging to a man I chose will sprout. Next day, Moses entered the tent and found that Aaron's staff, which represented the house of Levi had not only sprouted but, had budded, blossomed and produced almonds. All the tribes accepted defeat (Numbers 17:1 to 13).

24. Drinking water came out of a rock – When the Israelites arrived at the desert of Zin near Kadesh, Miriam died and was buried there. There was no drinking water and all Israelites quarreled with Moses and Aaron for water. As commanded by the Lord, Moses and Aaron went with all Israelites to a rock and Moses raised his arm and struck the rock twice with his staff instead of simply speaking to the rock, and water gushed out of the rock.

25. A bronze snake to make Israelites bitten by venomous snakes to live – Israelites travelled from Mount Hor and grew impatient and spoke against God and Moses. Lord sent venomous snakes among the Israelites and many of them died of snakebites. They all requested Moses to get rid of venomous snakes. Lord ordered Moses to make a bronze serpent and put it on a pole. Whoever was bitten by snakes, if he looked at this bronze snake he lived (Numbers 21:4 to 9).

26. Balaam's donkey spoke with its mouth to Balaam – When Balaam, was riding on his donkey but did what God did not like so, God was angry. The Lord stood in the form of an angel on the road with his sword drawn. The donkey saw the angel and fled from the road into a field. The donkey saw the angel thrice and Balaam had to beat the donkey. At last, the donkey opened its mouth and spoke to Balaam. Then, Balaam opened his

eyes and saw the angel of the Lord, who said that the donkey had no mistake but protected Balaam as God desired to oppose Balaam from his path (Numbers 22:21 to 35).

27. Water in the upstream of Jordan river stopped and all Israelites could cross the river to reach Jericho – After Moses died on Mount Nebo in Jordan, Joshua led the Israelites and asked the priests to carry the Ark of the Covenant in front of all Israelites and as their feet touched the water in river Jordan, the upstream water stopped, giving a dry land for all Israelites to cross river Jordan and reach Jericho (Joshua 3:1 to 17).

28. The walls of Jericho city collapsed and Israelites entered Jericho city – As ordered by the Lord, Joshua made the priests to carry the Ark in front of the seven priests carrying trumpets with armed men and circled round Jericho city once a day for six days and on the seventh day, they circled seven times and trumpets sounded and when Joshua ordered, all of them shouted, and the walls of Jericho city collapsed. The soldiers killed everyone, except Rahab's family (Joshua 6:1 to 21).

29. The sun stood still in the sky for a full day – Joshua with all the army marched all night from Gilgal to Gibeon and as the enemies fled from Beth Horon to Azekah and Makkedah, the Lord hurled large hail stones down on them from the sky and many died by these stones than by the swords of Israelites. Joshua said to the Lord in the presence of Israelites to stop the sun for the whole day over Gibeon and the moon over the valley of Aijalon and the Joshua and armies killed all enemies (Joshua 10:7 to 15).

30. Samson killed a lion with his hands – Samson went down to Timnah with his father and mother to see his proposed wife. As they approached the vineyards of Timnah, suddenly, a young lion came roaring towards

them. Samson with the help of the Lord tore the lion apart with his bare hands (Judges 14:4 to 7).

31. God opened up the hollow place in Lehi and water came out of it for Samson to drink – As Samson approached Lehi, the Philistines came upon him. Samson found a fresh jawbone of a donkey and killed a thousand Philistines. Samson was thirsty and prayed to the Lord, when God opened up the hollow place in Lehi and water came out of it for Samson to drink (Judges 15:13 to 19).

32. The statue of Philistines God Dagon fell on its face twice before the Ark of the Covenant – The Philistines captured the Ark of the Covenant and carried it to Ashdod and placed it by the side of the statue of their God Dagon. When they rose in the morning, they observed for two days, that the Dagon had fallen on its face and its head and hands had been broken. So, the Philistines transferred the Ark to Gath, then to Ekron and after seven months, the Ark was returned by Philistines to Israelites (I Samuel 5:1 to 12 and Chapter 6:1 to 21).

33. Seventy men of Beth Shemesh were put to death for looking into the Ark of Covenant – As the Ark of the Covenant was coming from Philistines to Israelites, the People of Beth Shemesh looked into the Ark and God struck seventy of them (I Samuel 6:19 to 20).

34. The Lord thundered with loud thunder against Philistines and threw them into panic. – Philistines heard that Israelites assembled at Mizpah and attacked them. Samuel sacrificed a burnt offering to save Israelites and the Lord thundered with a loud thunder against Philistines and threw them into panic, and the Israelites slaughtered them (I Samuel 7:7 to 11).

35. The Lord sent thunder and rain at the time of wheat harvest – The people asked Samuel that they wanted a

king to rule over them. But Samuel said, that they had the Lord as their king and said that for the evil thing they asked he would ask God to send thunder and rain, and it happened like that, and the people realized their mistake in asking for a king (I Samuel 12:12 to 19).

36. Sound of marching of armies in the tops of Balsam trees – The Philistines once again came in the valley of Rephaim. The Lord told David to attack them in front of balsam trees and as soon as David heard the sound of marching of soldiers in the tops of balsam trees, which meant that Lord was in front of them, David struck down the Philistines (II Samuel 5:22 to 25).

37. When the Ark of the Covenant was being brought on a cart, drawn by oxen, the oxen stumbled and Uzzah, who was on the cart reached out and took hold of the Ark from falling. Lord burned against Uzzah for this irrelevant action and struck him and he died by the side of the Ark (II Samuel 6:1 to 7).

38. King Jeroboam's hand withered and the new Altar he built was split apart – King Jeroboam offered sacrifices on the altar he had built at Bethel. By the word of the Lord, a man of God came to Bethel and cried out against the altar as Jeroboam was at the altar with an offering. Jeroboam stretched forth his hand and said, "Seize him." But the hand was withered and he could not pull it back. After the man of God prayed, his hand was made normal (I Kings 13:1 to 6).

39. Prophet Elijah was fed by the ravines every day with bread and meat in the Kerith Ravine, east of Jordan (I Kings17:1 to 6).

40. A widow at Zarephath had a jar of flour and jug of oil with very little flour and oil. Elijah was fed by her and the flour and oil did not get exhausted (I Kings 17:7-16).

41. Son of the widow at Zarephath died and Elijah raised him – The son of the widow who was feeding prophet Elijah was ill, and died. The widow was unhappy with Elijah. But he took the boy to his upper room and cried to God by stretching himself on the boy thrice. The boy was alive and Elijah handed him over to his mother, who then believed that Elijah was really a man of God (I Kings 17:17 to 24).

42. On Mount Carmel Elijah proved before four hundred fifty prophets of their God Baal and 450 prophets of Asherah that the Lord God was real the God, as he sent fire from heaven and consumed the burnt offering – One bull was cut and set on wood by all the Prophets of Baal, and one was cut by Elijah and put separately. The prophets of Baal called their God till afternoon, dancing and singing but the offering was not consumed by fire from heaven. Then, Elijah made his altar drenched with water three times. He, then, prayed to the Lord and his prayer was answered, as fire from heaven came down and completely consumed the offering including the wood, water, stones and every-thing there. Then Elijah asked the people to seize all the prophets of Baal, and kill them (I Kings 18:16 to 40).

43. The wall collapsed on the twenty seven thousand Aramean soldiers and killed them all – The Arameans thought that the Lord God of Israelites was the God of hills and not the God of valleys. For seven days, the armies of Arameans and Israelites camped opposite to each other and on the seventh day, Israelites killed hundred thousand soldiers of Arameans and the rest escaped to the city of Aphek, where the wall collapsed on the twenty seven thousand Aramean soldiers, and killed them (I Kings 20:28 to 30).

44. Fire from heaven consumed the two captains of King Ahaziah and fifty men following each captain, and King Ahaziah died according to the Lord's command

- King Ahaziah had fallen from the lattice of his upper room in Samaria, and was injured. He sent messengers to consult Baal-Zebub, the God of Ekron to see whether he would recover from the injury. Prophet Elijah met the messengers and told them that their king will die with his injury. When the messengers told King Ahaziah the words of Elijah, the king sent a captain with fifty men twice to Elijah and both the times, they were all consumed by fire from heaven. The third time, as ordered by the Lord, Elijah went to the King Ahaziah with the captain and told the king that he would die, and accordingly King Ahaziah died (II Kings Chapter 1)

45. Prophet Elijah rolled up his cloak and struck the water of river Jordan, when the water got separated and both prophets Elijah and Elisha crossed the dry land of river Jordan – Prophet Elijah kept Prophet Elisha at a place and went to Bethel, Jericho and Jordan as the Lord had sent him. Fifty men of the company of these prophets were standing at a distance and watching. Prophet Elijah rolled his cloak and struck the water of river Jordan and water got separated, leaving a dry land for both Elijah and Elisha to cross the river Jordan (II Kings 2:1 to 7).

46. Suddenly, a chariot of fire and horses of fire appeared and separated Elijah and Elisha, and Elijah went up to heaven in a whirlwind – After crossing the dry land of river Jordan, Elijah and Elisha were walking together, when Elisha asked Elijah to give him a double portion of his spirit. As they were walking, suddenly a chariot of fire and horses of fire appeared and separated the two of them, and Elijah went up to heaven in a whirlwind. Elisha saw this and cried. Elisha tore his own clothes. He took the cloak that had fallen down from Elijah as he went up to heaven. Elisha struck the water of river Jordan with the cloak of Elijah

remembering him, and the water got separated giving dry land for Elisha to cross the river. The fifty men went a round for three days to find out whether Elijah had come to any mountain or valley but, could not find him and came back and told Elisha (II Kings 2:9 to 18).

47. Prophet Elisha stayed at Jericho, when the people of Jericho complained to him that the water there was unproductive. Elisha threw salt in the spring of water and the water was healed and became productive (II Kings 2:19 to 22). This is now known as "Elisha Spring."

48. Two bears came out of the woods as ordered by the Lord and killed forty-two youth who ridiculed Elisha – As Prophet Elisha was walking along the road in Bethel, some youth came out of the town and ridiculed him, saying, "Go on up, you baldhead." Elisha turned round and looked at them and called down a curse on them in the name of the Lord. Then, two bears came out of woods and killed forty-two of the youth (II Kings 2:23 to 25).

49. As ordered by the Lord and said by Prophet Elisha, the valley was full of water without any wind or rain – The Kings of Israel, Jehoshapat the King of Judah and the King of Edom went to meet Prophet Elisha, who wanted a harpist. When the harpist was playing, the hand of the Lord came upon Elisha, who said that without wind or rain, this valley will be filled with water for you and for your cattle to drink. Thus, the armies of Moabites could be struck by these three kings (II Kings 3:13 to 26).

50. A widow asked Prophet Elisha to help her, as the creditors were threatening to take her two sons as slaves. She said that she had nothing at all in her house except a little oil. Elisha asked her to go a round and collect all empty jars and pour a little oil into each jar. She did as ordered by Prophet Elisha and all the jars

were filled with oil. Then, Prophet Elisha asked her to sell the oil and pay her debts (II Kings 4:1 to 7).

51. A woman from Shunem, who looked after Elisha very well was blessed with a son (II Kings 4:8 to 17).

52. The son of the Shunammite woman died. She carried him on a donkey all the way to Mount Carmel, where Prophet Elisha was staying. Elisha asked a man who was with him to place his staff on the boy. But, the boy did not wake up. On hearing this, Elisha himself went, stretched himself on the boy mouth to mouth, eyes to eyes, hands to hands, when the boy's body became warm and he sneezed seven times, and opened his eyes (II Kings 4:18 to 36).

53. Stew made by the servant of Elisha for the guests was poisonous, as the servant mixed gourds of wild vine in it. But when the guest complained, Elisha mixed some flour into the stew and made it non harmful (II Kings 4:38 to 41).

54. Elisha made twenty loaves of barley brought by a man to be served to one hundred men, and they ate, and some were remaining (II Kings 4:42 to 44).

55. Naaman, a commander of the army of the King of Aram was struck with leprosy. When Naaman came to Elisha, he sent a messenger to tell Naaman to go and wash seven times in river Jordan and get cured. Naaman was not happy, as Elisha himself did not meet him. But, as advised by Elisha and persuaded by elders, Naaman went and washed himself seven times in river Jordan and his skin became fresh as a young boy (II Kings 5:1 to 14).

56. Prophet Elisha made an iron axe fall into river Jordan and made it float on water – The company of Prophets said to Prophet Elisha to accompany them to go to Jordan and make a place for them to live. They started

cutting wood by the side of river Jordan and the axe of one of them fell into the water. The man told Prophet Elisha that it was a borrowed axe. Elisha asked him where the axe had fallen. On showing the place, Elisha threw a small piece of stick and the iron axe floated, and was picked up (II Kings 6:1 to 7).

57. When the Aramean armies surrounded the place where Prophet Elisha was staying, Elisha prayed to the Lord to make them all blind, and accordingly they became blind. Elisha misguided them, and made them enter Samaria. Elisha did not allow the King of Israel to kill them, but made a great feast for them and sent them away to their land safely (II Kings 6:8 to 23).

58. Elisha died and was buried. Once, while some Israelites were burying a man, suddenly they saw a band of Moabite raiders. So, they threw the dead body of the man into Elisha's tomb. When the dead body touched Elisha's bones, the dead man came to life and stood up on his feet (II Kings 13:20 to 21).

59. Prophet Isaiah prophesied the fall of Sennacherib, King of Assyria. One night, the angel of the Lord went out and put to death a hundred and eighty five thousand men of Assyrian camp. When the people got up the next morning, there were all the dead bodies. So, Sennacherib, the King of Assyria broke the camp and withdrew. He returned to Nineveh and stayed there (II Kings 19:35 to 36).

60. The shadow of the sun goes back ten degrees on the sundial of Ahaz (II Kings 20:9 to 11).

61. King Uzziah was struck with leprosy for disobeying all the priests – King Uzziah became powerful and he became unfaithful to the Lord his God. He entered the temple to burn incense on the altar. Azariah the priest with eighty other courageous priests entered the

temple and advised Uzziah not to do that. He became very angry with all the priests, but he was struck with leprosy on his forehead. He had leprosy till he died (II Chronicles 26:16 to 21).

62. King Nebuchadnezzar, the King of Babylon was furious with the men of the Lord, Shadrach, Meshach and Abednego and ordered that they should be thrown into a furnace. But, the Lord God protected them and they were not burnt at all – King Nebuchadnezzar made an image of gold, ninety feet high and nine feet wide and set it on the plain of Dura in his province of Babylon. The king called all governors, chiefs and all people and got it announced that as soon as the music was played, everyone should fall down and worship the image of gold and whoever failed to do so, would be thrown in to a blazing furnace. But, some people of Babylon reported to King Nebuchadnazzer that the three jews, Shadrach, Meshach and Abednego did not worship the golden image. The king was very furious and asked his people to make the furnace seven times hoter and these three men were tied and thrown into the furnace. Next morning, the king found four people moving in the furnace without being burnt. The fourth one was like a son of the God. The king approached the furnace and shouted, "Shadrach, Meshach and Abednego, servants of the Most High God, come out, come here." When they came out, they observed that not a single hair of them was burnt. The king praised the God of these three jews (Daniel 3:1 to 30).

63. Daniel was thrown by King Darius into the den of lions, but he was not touched by the lions – King Darius ruled, after King Nebuchadnezzer. They made King Darius come out with a rule that for the next thirty days, no one should pray to any God except King Darius and any one disobeying it will be thrown into the den of lions. Daniel prayed three times a day to his God, as

usual. The people reported to the king and he ordered that Daniel should be thrown into the den of lions. The king could not eat or sleep that night. Early morning, he went to the den of lions and called, "Daniel, servant of the living God, has your God rescued you from the lions?" Daniel answered, "O King, my God sent his angels to shut the mouths of the lions." The king ordered Daniel should be brought out and the men who falsely accused Daniel should be thrown into the den of lions with their families. Thus, God saved Daniel even from ferocious lions (Daniel 6:1 to 24).

64. The Lord made a large fish swallow Jonah, who was thrown into the sea and Jonah was in the belly of the fish for three days and three nights – God asked Jonah to go to the city of Nineveh and preach to them. But, Jonah did not want to go to Nineveh and went to the port city of Joppa and entered a ship going to Tarshish. The Lord sent a great wind on the sea and the ship was in danger of breaking down. But, Jonah went to the deck of the ship and was fast asleep. The sailors woke him up and after enquiring from him, they found that he disobeyed God and he was responsible for the storm. They all threw Jonah into the sea. But, the Lord made a big fish swallow Jonah and he was in the belly of the fish for three days and three nights. Jonah prayed to God from the belly of the fish. God commanded the fish to vomit Jonah on dry land. Then, Jonah repented and went to Nineveh, as God desired (Jonah chapter 1 and 2).

8.

Forty Parables in the Four Gospels of the New Testament, in Serial Order

There are forty Parables mentioned in the four Gospels.

1. Matthew

Once, the disciples of the Jesus Christ came to him and asked, "Why do you speak to the people in parables?"

Jesus replied, "The knowledge of the secrets of the kingdom of heaven has been given to you, but not to them. Whoever has will be given more, and he will have abundance. Who ever does not have, even what he has will be taken from him. This is why I speak to them in parables" (Matthew 13:10 to 11).

These forty parables are explained briefly in the following pages:-

1. The Parable of a Farmer sowing Seeds – "A farmer went out to sow his seeds and some fell along the path and the birds ate them, some fell on rocky places and they withered away as they had no roots, some fell among thorns which choked the plants and some fell on good soil and produced a crop – a hundred, sixty or thirty

times what was sown. He who has ears let him hear" (Mt. 13:3 to 9) (Mark 4:1 to 8).

2. The Parable of the Weeds among Good Seeds – Jesus said, "The kingdom of heaven is like a man who sowed good seeds in the field. But, while everyone was sleeping, his enemy came and sowed weeds among the wheat and went away. When the wheat sprouted and formed heads, then the weeds also appeared. The man asked his servants to allow the weeds also to grow and at the time of harvest, the weeds could be collected first and burnt and then the wheat" (Mt. 13:23 to 30).

3. The Parable of the Mustard Seed – Jesus said, "The kingdom of heaven is like a mustard seed, which a man took and planted in his field. Though the mustard seed is the smallest of all the seeds, yet when it grows, it is the largest of garden plants and becomes a tree, so that the birds of the air come and rest on its branches" (Mt. 13:31 to 32) (Mark 4:30 to 32).

4. The Parable of the Yeast – Jesus said, "The kingdom of heaven is like yeast that a woman took and mixed into a large amount of flour until it worked all through the dough" (Mt. 13:33).

5. The Parable of the Hidden Treasure – Jesus said, "The kingdom of heaven is like – treasure hidden in a field. When a man found it, he hid it again and then in his joy went and sold all he had and bought the field" (Mt. 13:44).

6. The Parable of the Pearls – Jesus said, "The kingdom of heaven is like a merchant looking for fine pearls. When he found one of great value, he went away and sold everything he had and bought it" (Mt. 13:45 and 46).

7. The Parable of a Net to catch Fish – Jesus said, "The kingdom of heaven is like a net that was let down into the lake and caught all kinds of fish. When it was full,

the fishermen pulled it up on the shore. Then, they sat down and collected the good fish in baskets, but threw away the bad fish. This is how it will be at the end of the age. The angels will come and separate the wicked from the righteous and throw the wicked into the fiery furnace, where there will be weeping and gnashing of teeth" (Mt. 13:47 to 50).

8. The Parable of the unmerciful Servant – Jesus said, "A king wanted to settle his account with his servants. One man owed ten thousand talents but he could not pay and begged for mercy. The king cancelled his debt. But, this servant went out and found his fellow servant who owed him a small amount of hundred denarii's and got him thrown into prison till he paid it. When the king heard this he called the first servant and asked why he could not have mercy as he had on him and he got him put into jail." Jesus said, "This is how my heavenly father will treat each of you unless you forgive your brother from your heart" (Mt. 18:21 to 35).

9. The Parable of the workers in the Vineyard – Jesus said, "For the kingdom of heaven is like a landlord who went early in the morning to hire men to work in his vineyard. He agreed to pay them a denarius's for the day. Like that, he sent other labourers at the third hour, sixth hour and eleventh hour also. At the end of the day, he called his servant and asked him to pay equal amount of one denarius's to all of them. But, those who came early grumbled, when they saw that those who came in the last hour also were paid the same amount. But, the landlord said, "Did you not agree with me for one danarius, take it and go, Am I not at liberty to do what I want with my own money? So, the last will be first and the first will be last." (Mt. 20:1 to 16).

10. The Parable of the Two Sons of a Man – Jesus said, "There was a man who had two sons. He asked the first son to go in to his vineyard and work. But, the son

first refused, but later on changed his mind and went to the vineyard to work. The father went to his second son and asked him to go to the vineyard and work. He said that he would go, but did not go. So, which of the two did what his father wanted? The people answered, "The first son." Jesus said, that "John the Baptist came to show the way of righteousness but you did not believe in him" (Mt. 21:28 to 32).

11. The parable of a Wedding Banquet of a king's Son – Jesus said, "The kingdom of heaven is like a king's wedding banquet for his son. After the dinner was prepared on a grand scale he sent his servant to bring the guests, but all of them refused to come on some pretext. The king was enraged. He asked his servants to go into the streets and call everyone. So, the servants did so and the wedding hall was full with guests. For many are invited, but a few are chosen." (Mt. 22:1 to 14).

12. The Parable of the Tenants who were Bad – Jesus said, "There was a landowner, who planted a vineyard and went away on a journey. When the harvest time approached, he sent his servants one after the other and at last his only son to collect his fruit. But, the tenants killed all of them." Jesus asked the people, "What will the owner of vineyard do to those tenants?" (Mt. 21:33 to 40) (Mark 12:1 to 12).

13. The Parable of the Ten Virgins in a Wedding – Jesus said, "No one knows the time when He would come again. At that time, the kingdom of heaven will be like ten virgins who took their lamps and went to meet the bridegroom. Five were wise with extra oil for the lamps, and five were foolish with no oil. While the coming of the bridegroom was delayed, they all slept. At midnight, the bridegroom came and the lamps of the foolish virgins could not be lighted, as there was no oil. The wise virgins could not spare their oil. When

the wise virgins went in with the bridegroom: the door was shut and the foolish virgins could not enter. Therefore, keep watch, because you do not know the day and hour of His coming" (Mt. 25:1 to 13).

14. The Parable of Talents given by a Master to his Servants – Jesus said, "A man going on a journey called his servants and gave five talents, two talents and one talent each. When he returned, he called his servants to know how much they made. The men who got five and two talents earned double the money they got. The man who got one talent did not earn anything, knowing that his master was a hard man. The master was angry and asked him to be thrown outside, where there will be weeping and gnashing of teeth"(Mt. 25:14 to 30).

15. The Parable of Sheep and Goats – Jesus said, "When the son of man comes in his glory and all angels with him, he will sit on his throne in heavenly glory. He will separate people one from another, as a shepherd separates the sheep from the goats (Mt. 25:31 to 46).

2. *Mark*

16. The Parable of the Seed Sprouting and Growing – Jesus said that "The kingdom of God is like a man sowing his seed and whether he sleeps or gets up, the seed sprouts and grows without his knowledge. When the corn is ready, he harvests the crop" (Mark 4:26 to 29).

17. The Parable of the coming of the House Owner – Jesus said, "No one knows about that day or hour when He comes, except the Father. So, be on guard, be alert and be watchful always" (Mark 13:32 to 37).

3. *Luke*

18. Parable of two Debtors – Jesus said to Simon, "Two men owed money to a certain moneylender. One owed

him five hundred denarii's and the other fifty. Neither of them had the money to pay back. So, he cancelled the debts of both. Now, which of them will love him more?" Simon said that the one who had a bigger debt. Jesus said, "Many sins of the woman who anointed me are forgiven, for she loved much. But, he who has been forgiven little loves little" (Luke 7:41 to 47).

19. The Parable of the Good Samaritan – When a man asked, who is my neighbour? Jesus said, "A man was going from Jerusalem to Jericho. He fell in the hands of robbers, who took everything and threw him away by roadside. A priest and a levite went that way, but did not care for the man. A Samaritan came there and took pity on him and got him admitted into an inn, and paid all his expenses. So, who among of the three is a neighbour?" The man replied, "The Samaritan." Jesus said, "Go and do likewise" (Chapter 10:25 to 37).

20. The Parable of a Friend at Midnight – Jesus said, "Suppose you have a friend, who comes at midnight and asks for three loaves of bread to feed another friend and goes on asking, you will get up from your bed and give him as much as he wants. Ask and it will be given to you" (Luke 11:5 to 9).

21. The Parable of a Rich Fool – Jesus said, "A rich man had a good harvest and he said to himself be happy, drink and be merry. But God said to him, you fool, this very night your life will be demanded from you and what will happen to all your riches? So, anyone who stores up things for himself and not rich towards God will have the same fate" (Ch 12:13 to 21).

22. The Parable of Watchful Servant – Jesus said, "If the owner of a house knows at what time the thief is coming, his house cannot be broken. Thus, you must also be ready, because the son of man will come at an hour when you do not expect him" (Ch 12:35 to 40).

23. The Parable of a Wise Manager – Jesus said, "If a servant in charge of other servants thinks that his master is taking a long time to come and starts beating other servants and gets drunk, the master would come unexpectedly and punish him" (Ch 12:42 to 48).

24. The Parable of a Barren Fig Tree – Jesus said, "A man had a fig tree and for three years, there were no figs. He asked his gardener to cut it down. But the gardener said, give one more year as he would fertilize it and if it does not give figs, it could be cut down (Ch 13:6 to 9).

25. The Parable of Great Banquet – Jesus said that "A man made a great banquet and invited many guests. But at the time of dinner, every guest made excuses. The man was angry and asked his servants to go into the streets and bring everyone in the streets, as the invited guests are not worthy" (Ch 14:15 to 24).

26. The Parable of a Tower Construction and its Cost – Jesus said, "If one wants to construct a tower, he will have to first make an estimate of the cost and see if he has enough money to complete it. Otherwise, if he stops the tower construction in the middle, everyone will ridicule him" (Ch 14:28 to 30).

27. The Parable of the Lost Sheep – Jesus said, "Suppose one has hundred sheep and loses one of them, he would leave the ninety nine sheep in open area and go after that which was lost. Then, when he finds it, he will rejoice. Thus, there will be joy over one sinner that repenteth than ninety nine righteous persons, who do not need to repent" (Ch 15:4 to 7).

28. The Parable of a Lost Coin – Jesus said, "Suppose a woman had ten silver coins and loses one. She will light a lamp, sweep the house in search of the coin and when she finds it, she will rejoice. Thus, there is rejoicing in the presence of angels of God over one sinner who repents" (Ch 15:8 to 10).

29. The Parable of Prodigal Son – Jesus said, "There was man who had two sons. The youngest son fought for his share of property and took it and went to distant country and wasted the money with his friends. They had no money left, so he went to a man, who asked him to look after his pigs. Out of hunger, he had to eat what the pigs ate. One day, he repented and went back to his father with the same dirty clothes, Father recognized him from a distance and went and kissed him and had a great feast as his son was lost but found. But his elder brother was angry as this boy had wasted the money and had now come back. But the father consoled him by saying they must rejoice, as his son was dead and now alive again, he was lost and now found" (Ch 15:11 to 31).

30. The Parable of a Shrewd Manager – There was a rich man, who had a manager accused of wasting his possessions. The rich man called the manager and told him that he cannot be a manager anymore, so he had to give account. This shrewd manager called all the debtors of the rich man and made them all write less debt in their bonds. The rich man commended this dishonest manager, because he had acted shrewdly (Ch 16:1 to 12).

31. The Parable of the Rich Man and Poor Lazarus – Jesus said, "There was a rich man and a poor man, Lazarus who sat at the gate waiting for any leftover food. When Lazarus died, the angels carried him to Abraham's side. The rich man also died and he went to hell. He saw Abraham with Lazarus by his side and cried to send Lazarus with his finger dipped in water to cool his tongue. But Abraham replied that once he was rich and Lazarus was poor and there was a huge wall in between them and none could cross. The rich man said send Lazarus to his father's house and warn his five brothers. But Abraham said there are prophets and if they do

not hear them, they will not hear even if Lazarus goes there (Ch 16:19 to 31).

32. The Parable of a Servant Plowing – Jesus said that "Suppose one of you had a servant ploughing or looking after the sheep, would you ask him to sit down and eat with you. So, you also, when you have done everything you have been told to do say, we are unworthy servants, we have only done our duty" (Ch 17:7 to 10).

33. The Parable of the Persistent Widow – Jesus wanted to tell his disciples that they should always pray and not give up. Jesus said, "There was a judge who never cared for any one. In that place, there was a widow visiting the judge asking him to grant justice against her enemy. He was tired of the persistent visits of the widow and to stop her coming, he heard her. Similarly, God will bring about justice for all his chosen ones, who cry out to him day and night" (Ch 18:1 to 8).

34. The Parable of the Pharisee and the Tax Collector – Jesus said, "Two men went up to a temple to pray, one a Pharisee and the other a tax collector. The Pharisee stood up and prayed saying – "God, I thank you that I am not like other men – robbers, evil doers, adulterers or even as this tax collector. I fast twice a week and give a tenth of all I get." But, the tax collector stood at a distance and could not even look up to heaven, but beat his breast and said – "God have mercy on me, a sinner." Jesus said, "This tax collector went home justified rather than the other Pharisee. For every one who exalts himself will be humbled and he who humbles himself will be exalted" (Ch 18:9 to 14).

35. The Parable of the Ten Minas – Jesus said, "A noble man was going to a distant country and he called ten of his servants and gave them ten minas each and told them to put the minas to work and earn more. When

he returned, he called them one by one. The first said that he had gained ten more minas. The man appreciated and made him incharge of ten cities. The second servant came and said that he had earned five more minas for the five minas given by him. This servant was given charge of five cities. Another servant came and said that you are a hard master, so I have kept the minas given by you in a piece of cloth and preserved it. The master was angry and said why did you not deposit in a bank and I could have taken it with interest. The master ordered that these minas should be given to the one who has ten minas. Thus, one who has more will have more and one who has nothing; even what he has will be taken away from him (Ch 19:12 to 27).

36. Wise man built his house on a rock and foolish man on sand – Jesus said that whosoever heareth his sayings and doeth them is like a wise man who built his house on a rock and even after rains and floods, it did not fall. But whosoever did not follow his words was like a foolish man who built his house on sand and when rain and floods came, it fell (Matthew 7:24 to 27, Luke 6:48 and 49).

37. A lighted candle is put on candlestick to give light – Jesus said, "Ye are the light of the world, a city that is set on a hill cannot be hid. No man can keep a lighted candle under a bushel, but on a candlestick and it giveth light unto all that are in the house. Let your light so shine before men, that they may see your good works and glorify your Father, which is in heaven (Matthew 5:14 to 16; Mark 4:21 and 22; Luke 8:16 and 17).

38. Piece of new cloth is not stitched to old cloth and new wine is not poured into old bottles – Jesus said that the days would come when the bridegroom is taken away from them and then his disciples will fast. Jesus spoke

a parable to them saying that no man putteth a piece of new garment upon an old as the new agreeth not with old and both will tear off. No man putteth new wine into old bottles, as the bottle will break. New wine should be put in new bottles only (Matthew 9:15 to 17; Mark 2:18 to 22; Luke 5:34 to 39).

39. A certain man planted a vineyard, let it to husbandmen and went to a far off country. At the time of the harvest of grapes, he sent his servants one after another, to collect his share of grapes. But, husbandmen killed some and wounded some and sent them away empty handed. At last, the owner sent his only son, thinking that he will be respected. But the husbandmen killed him also, as he was the heir. The owner therefore destroyed the wicked husbandmen and gave the vineyard to others (Matthew 21:33 to 41; Mark 12: 1 to 9 and Luke 20:9 to 16).

40. Tender leaves of a fig tree indicate oncoming of summer – Jesus said that the tender leaves of a fig tree indicate the oncoming of summer. When ye see all these things, you know that the son of man is coming with power (Mt. 24:32 to 35; Mark 13:28 to 31; Luke 21:29 to 31).

9.

Thirty Five Miracles in the Four Gospels of the New Testament, in Serial Order

A total number of thirty five miracles performed by Jesus Christ have been recorded in the four gospels of the New Testament. These are explained in the following pages :-

1. A man with leprosy healed – when Jesus came down from the mountain, a man with leprosy came and knelt before him and said, "Lord, if you are willing, you can make me clean." Jesus stretched out his hand and touched him, saying, "I am willing, be thou clean." Immediately, he was cured. (Mt. 8:1 to 4, Mark 1:40, Luke 5:12 to 20).

2. Centurion's servant cured of paralysis – when Jesus entered Capernaum, a centurion came and asked Jesus to cure his servant, who was suffering from paralysis. Jesus said that he would go to the centurion's house. But, the centurion said "I am not worthy to receive you in my house, but just say a word and he will be cured." Jesus was surprised at the faith of the centurion and healed his servant. (Mt. 8: 5-1. Luke 7: 2 to 10).

3. Peter's mother-in-law was cured of fever- when Jesus came to Peter's house in Capernaum, she was having

fever. Jesus touched her hand and the fever left her. (Mt. 8: 5 to 13, Mark 1: 30 -31, Luke 5: 38 and 39).

4. Jesus calms the storm on the sea of Galilee- Jesus got into a boat along with his disciples to go to the other side of the sea. A furious storm came, but Jesus was sleeping in the boat. The disciples woke him up saying, "Lord, save us! We are going to drown! "Jesus got up and rebuked the winds and waves, which became calm (Mt. 8:23 to 27, Mark 4:35-41 Luke 8:22-25).

5. Healing two men possessed by demon – when Jesus arrived at the other side in the region of Gadarenes, two men possessed by demons came out of the tombs and met Jesus. They asked Jesus to send them into a herd of swine feeding nearby. The demons entered the pigs, which ran into the nearby sea and got drowned. The two men were healed (Mt. 8: 23 to 34, Mark 5: 1 -14 Luke 8: 26-39).

6. Jesus healed a man affected with paralysis- when Jesus stepped out of the boat and came to his own town, some men brought a person having paralysis lying on a mat. When Jesus saw their faith, he asked the person to take up his mat go home and he went home (Mt. 9:2 to 8, Mark 2:3 to 12 and Luke 5: 18 to 26).

7. A certain ruler (Jairus) came to Jesus and worshipped him saying, "My daughter is even now dead, but come lay thy hand upon her, and she shall live." Jesus followed him along with his disciples. When he came to the house, all were making noise and Jesus said that the girl was sleeping. They all laughed at Jesus. But, Jesus took her by hand and she arose (Mt. 8:18 to 19 and 23 to 25, Mark 5: 22 to 24 and 35-43, Luke 8: 41 to 42 and 51 to 56).

8. A woman, who had issue of blood for twelve years touched the hem of Jesus' garment as he was going to Jairus's house. Jesus said, "Daughter, be of good

comfort, thy faith hath made thee whole" She was healed (Mt. 9:20 to22, Mark 5:25-34, Luke 8:43to 48).

9. Two blind men received their sight- As Jesus went on, two blind men followed him calling out, "Have mercy on us, son of David." Jesus touched their eyes and they received their sight (Mt. 9:27 to 31).

10. Jesus healed a mute man possessed by demon. – A man, who was possessed by a demon and could not speak (mute) was brought to Jesus. Jesus drove out the demon and the man could speak (Mt. 9:32to 34).

11. Jesus healed a man with whithered hand –Jesus went into a synagogue on a Sabbath day. There was a man with whithered hand, Jesus said, "Stretch forth your hand." He stretched it and was completely healed (Mt. 12:10-13, Mark 3:1 to 5; 6 to 10).

12. Jesus healed a man possessed by a demon who was blind and mute-Jesus healed him and he could see and speak also (Mt. 12:22, Luke 11 :14)

13. Jesus fed five thousand men with five loaves and two fishes - In the evening, Jesus saw a large crowd and he had compassion on them. Jesus asked his disciples to give them something to eat. His disciples said that there was a boy who had five loaves and two fishes. Jesus blessed the fish and bread and his disciple served them to five thousand people and after they ate, the disciples collected twelve baskets full remnants (Mt. 14: 13 to 21; Mark 6:34 to 44, Luke 9:12 to 17 , John 6:1 to 14)

14. Jesus walked on the Sea of Galilee –Jesus made his disciples get into a boat ahead of him. As the wind was strong, the disciple had some trouble in rowing the boat. Jesus walked on the sea and reached the boat and the wind stopped. The disciples were amazed at this (Mt. 14: 22 to 27, Mark 6: 45 to 51).

15. Jesus healed the daughter of a Cananite woman having great faith-when Jesus went to Tyre and Sidon, a Cananite woman met Jesus and cried, saying that her daughter was possessed by demon and desired that Jesus should heal her. Jesus said, "It is not right to take the children's bread and give it to the dog." But, the woman said, "Yes sir, but the dog also eats crumbs that fall from their master's table." Jesus appreciated her faith and healed her daughter (Mt. 15:21 to 28, Mark 7:24 to 30).

16. Jesus fed four thousand people with seven loaves and few small fishes-Jesus went along the Sea of Galilee and went up to a mountain and sat down. A great crowd came to him bringing people having all kinds of sickness and Jesus healed them all. In the evening, Jesus said to his disciples, " I have compassion for these people , as they were with me for three days and have nothing to eat. How many loaves do you have?" The disciples said, "Seven loaves and a few small fishes." Jesus blessed the loaves and fishes and the disciples served them to all the people, which were about four thousand men. After they all ate, the disciples gathered seven baskets full of remnants (Mt. 15:32 to 39, Mark 8: 1 to 10).

17. Jesus healed a boy possessed by demon -A man approached Jesus and asked him to heal his son possessed by a demon, which often threw him in fire or water, but the disciple could not heal him. Jesus healed the boy in a moment. The disciple's asked Jesus as to why they couldn't heal the boy. Jesus said, "You have only little faith. If any one has faith as little as a mustard seed, he can see that a mountain is thrown into sea" (Mt. 17: 14 to 21, Mark 9: 17 to 29, Luke 9:38 to 43).

18. A coin in the mouth of the fish to pay temple tax for Jesus and Peter – when Jesus arrived at Capernaum with his disciples, a tax collector met Peter and asked

him, whether Jesus paid temple tax . Peter said, "Yes". Jesus knew it, and asked Peter to go to the lake and throw the hook; and take the first fish caught and open its mouth; and he would find a four-drachma coin and pay them toward Jesus' tax and Peter's tax (Mt. 17:24 to 27).

19. Jesus healed two blind men in Jericho-As Jesus was leaving Jericho, two blind men sitting by the roadside shouted, "Lord, son of David! have mercy on us ." Jesus had compassion on them and touched their eyes and they received their sight (Mt. 20: 29 to 34, Mark 10:46 to 52 Luke 18:35 to 43

20. Jesus healed a man possessed with an evil spirit –on a Sabbath day; Jesus went into a synagogue in Capernaum. A man possessed by an evil spirit cried out saying, "Let us alone, what have we to do with thee, thou Jesus of Nazareth? Art thou come to destroy us? I know thee who thou art, the Holy one of God." Jesus said, "Hold thy peace and come out of him "The man was healed.

21. Jesus healed a blind man in Bethsaida –When Jesus came to Bethsaida with his disciple, people brought a blind man and begged Jesus to touch him. Jesus healed him (Mark 8: 22 to 26).

22. Jesus healed a boy possessed with an evil spirit –A man said to Jesus, "I brought my son possessed by an evil spirit that has robbed him of his speech. But your disciples could not heal him." Jesus said, "everything is possible for him who believes." The man cried out, "I do believe, help me to overcome my unbelief." Jesus rebuked the evil spirit saying, "You deaf and mute spirit, I command you, come out of him and never enter him again." The spirit left him and Jesus took him by hand and handed him over to his father (Mark 9:17 to 27).

23. Jesus cursed a fig tree, which gave no fruit and it dried away –Jesus, entered Jerusalem sitting on a donkey, and the went to Bethany for the night along with his disciples. Next morning, as he was going to Jerusalem from Bethany, he was hungry and seeing a fig tree at a distance he went there to eat some fig but there were no figs on the tree. Jesus cursed the fig tree, saying, "May no one ever eat fruit from you again." His disciples heard it. When returning from Jerusalem to Bethany his disciples saw that fig tree had whithered away (Mark: 11:12 to 22).

24. Jesus helped to catch lot of fish –One day, Jesus got into a boat belonging to Simon and taught the multitudes from the boat. Afterward, Jesus asked Simon to let down his net to catch fish. But, Simon said that he had tried the whole night but there was no catch. But as suggested by Jesus, Simon let down the net and there was a big catch of fish and his net was about to break. Simon Peter fell on Jesus' knees. (Luke 5: 1 to 11).

25. Jesus raised the dead son of a widow in Nain-Jesus came to a town known as Nain. He saw a dead person being carried out, the only son of a widow. Jesus consoled her and asked the coffin bearers to stop. Jesus touched the coffin, and said, "young man, I say unto you, get up." The dead boy sat and began to speak. Jesus gave him to his mother (Luke 7:11 to 15).

26. Jesus healed a crippled woman on a Sabbath day- on one Sabbath day, Jesus was preaching in synagogue. There was a woman, who was crippled for eighteen years. Jesus said to her, "Women, you are set free from your infirmity." She was healed (Luke 13:10 to 17).

27. Jesus healed a man having dropsy diseases; on the Sabbath day Jesus went into the house of one chief of Pharisees to eat bread on a Sabbath day. There was a

man with dropsy disease. Jesus asked the lawyer and Pharisees saying, "It is lawful to heal on the Sabbath day? "All of them held their peace. But Jesus healed the man and sent him away (Luke 14:1 to 4)

28. Jesus healed ten persons having leprosy – On his way to Jerusalem, Jesus travelled along the border between Samaria and Galilee. As Jesus was entering a village, ten men having leprosy stood afar off and called out in a loud voice, "Jesus, Master, have pity on us," Jesus said to them, "Go, show yourself unto priests." As they went they were cleansed, but only one glorified God and fell down on Jesus' feet. He was a Samaritan (Luke 7:11 to 17).

29. Jesus fixed the ear cut off from a man, when Jesus was arrested in the garden of Gethsemane –when Jesus was praying in the garden of Gethsemane, a crowd accompanied by Judas Iscariot came to arrest Jesus. One of Jesus' followers struck the servant of the High Priest cutting off his right ear. Jesus touched the man's ear and healed him (Luke 22:47 to 51).

30. Jesus changed water into wine at the wedding in Cana– There was a wedding in Cana of Galilee where Jesus and his disciples and Jesus' mother were present. When the wine was exhausted, Jesus mother came to him and said that there was no wine. Jesus said to her, "Woman, what have I to do with thee? My hour has not yet come." Jesus asked the servants to fill up the water pots with water. They filled six pots up to their brim. Then Jesus said to them to draw and take it to the governor of the feast who tasted the water that was made wine. This is the first miracles that Jesus did (John 2:1 to 11).

31. Jesus healed the son of a royal official- Jesus again came to Cana of Galilee. A noble man met Jesus and told him that his son was seriously ill at Capernaum and requested Jesus to come and heal his son. Jesus said,

"Go thy way; thy son liveth." The noble man believed the word of Jesus and went his way. On his way, his servants met him and said that his son was alive. He realized that his son was healed at the same time when Jesus told him that he liveth. His entire family believed in Jesus (John 4:46-54).

32. Jesus healed at Bethesda pool, a man who was sick for thirty eight years –Jesus went to Jerusalem. Near the Sheep Gate, there was a pool, which in Aramic language was known as Bethesda. Here, a great number of disabled people were waiting for the movement of water in the pool by an angel once in a year and whosoever stepped into the water first was made whole of any disease. There was a man waiting there for thirty eight years. Jesus pitied him and asked him, "Do you want to get well?" The invalid man said that there was no one to put him in the pool, when the water was troubled by the angel. Jesus said "Get up, pick up your bed and walk." The man was cured and went away (John 5:1 to 16).

33. Jesus healed a man, who was blind from his birth - As Jesus went with his disciples, they saw a man who was born blind. The disciples asked Jesus, "Rabbi, who sinned, this man or his parents, that he was born blind?" Jesus replied saying "Neither this man nor his parents sinned. But the works of God should be manifest in him." Jesus made clay and applied to his eyes and asked the blind man to go and wash in the pool of Siloam. The blind man washed in the pool of Siloam and got his sight (John 9:1 to 7).

34. Jesus raised Lazarus who was dead at Bethany –Jesus was visiting Mary, her sister Martha and their brother Lazarus who were residing in Bethany. Once Lazarus was sick and died. Jesus was not there. Mary and Martha sent word to Jesus. Jesus came to Bethany and wept. Jesus prayed, and said, "Lazarus, come out!"

Lazarus became alive. All were surprised (John 11: 38 to 44).

35. Jesus made his disciples catch one hundred fifty three big fishes in their net- After resurrection; Jesus appeared to his disciples who were fishing in the Sea of Galilee. One day, early in the morning, Jesus was standing on the shore, but his disciples did not realise that it was Jesus. Jesus asked them whether they had any fish. They said, "No". Jesus asked them to cast the net on the right side of the boat. They did so and caught one hundred fifty three fishes. Then the disciples realized that he was Jesus (John 21:1 to 13).

10.

Miracles in the Acts of Apostles, Epistles, and Revelations

There are a number of miracles mentioned in the Acts of Apostles, Epistles and Revelations of the New Testament. Some of these miracles were performed by Peter, Paul and God. But, all of them are not being explained in this book, just to reduce the volume of the book. However, a few references alone are given below:-

1. **Acts of Apostles.**

    1. The outpouring of the Holy Spirit with the accompanying signs. (Acts Ch.2)

    2. The gift of tongues. (Acts 2:4 to 11:10:44-46)

    3. Lame man at the beautiful gate of the temple. (Acts Ch.3)

    4. Death of Ananias and Sapphira .(Act Ch. 5)

    5. Healing of sick in the streets by Peter, etc.(Acts 5:15 and 16)

    6. Prison opened for apostles by the angel. (Acts 5:19: 12: 7-11)

7. Stephen's dying vision of Christ. (Acts 7:55 and 56).

8. Unclean spirits cast out by Philip. (Act 8: 6and 7).

9. Christ's appearance to Saul on his way to Damascus (Acts 9: 3 22: 6: 26: 13-19).

10. Saul 's recovery of sight.(Acts 9:17 and 18: 22: 12 and 13)

11. Eneas healed of palsy by Peter. (Acts 9:33 and 34).

12. Rising of Dorcas to life by Peter. (Acts 9:40).

13. Vision of Cornelius. (Acts 10:3, 4, 30-32).

14. Vision of Peter (Acts Ch. 10 and 11).

15. Peter miraculously released from prison (Acts 12 :7-11)

16. Elymas stricken with blindness. (Acts 13 :11).

17. Healing of Cripple at Lystra. (Acts 14 :8 to 18).

18. Vision of "Man of Macedonia" seen by Paul. (Acts 16: 9).

19. Spirit of Divination cast out of a damsel by Paul (Acts 16: 16-18)

20. Earthquake at Philippi. (Acts 16: 25 and 26).

21. Special miracles wrought by Paul and Ephesus. (Acts 19: 11-12)

22. Evil spirit puts to flight Sceva's sons. (Acts 19:13 -16)

23. Raising of Eutychus to life by Paul. (Acts 20: 9-12).

24. Prophecies of Agabus. (Acts 11: 28:21:11).

25. Appearance of Christ to Paul . (Acts 9:3 :22:17 -21 : 23:11: 27: 23&24).

26. Paul unharmed by the viper (Acts 28:3-5).

27. Paul healed Publius father and other sick at Melita (Acts 28: 8).

2. *Miracles Mentioned in the Epistles and Revalation*

28. Miracles wrought by Paul and others (Roman 15: 18 and 19)

ICor 12: 9 and 19, 28-31, 14:18, Gal. 3:5, I Timothy 1:20).

29. Miracles of tongues. (I Cor 14:27-33).

30. Appearance of Christ after his resurrection (I Cor 15: 4-8).

31. Visions and revelations of Paul (II Cor 12:1-5 and 12).

32. Wonders of the world to come (i.e. Gospel times) Heb 2:4: 6:5.

33. The visions of John in Patmos (Rev 1: 10, 4 to end of book)

11.

The Ark of the Convenant, Tabernacle and Other Items of Worship

Israelites came out of bondage from Egypt and were led by Moses and Aaron and others through the desert after crossing the Red Sea. They reached in the third month, the desert of Sinai and camped before Mount Sinai. Moses was meeting God on Mount Sinai often, as God was telling Moses many things about Israelites (Exodus 19:1 to 25).

According to Exodus 24: 9 to 18, Moses, Aaron, Nadab and Abihu and seventy other elders of Israel went up the Mount Sinai, and saw the God of Israel. The Lord said to Moses, "Come up to me on the mountain, and stay there; I will give you two stone tablets with the law and commands I have written for instructing Israelites.

When Moses went up to the mountain, the cloud covered it and the glory of the Lord settled on Mount Sinai for six days, the cloud covered the mountain and on the seventh day, the Lord called Moses from within the clouds. Moses entered the cloud as he went up to the Mount Sinai. Moses stayed there for forty days and forty nights.

Chapter 25 explains how the Lord told Moses the full dimensions and details of the Ark of the Covenant and other items of worship, as indicated below:-

1. The Ark of the Covenant.
2. The Table,
3. The Lamb stand,
4. The Tabernacles
5. The Altar of burnt offering,
6. The Courtyard,
7. Oil for the Lampstand,
8. Priestly Garments,
9. The Ephod,
10. The Breast Plate,
11. Other Priestly Garments,
12. Consecration of Priests,
13. The Altar of Incense,
14. Atonment Money,
15. Basin for washing (Laver of Bronze).
16. Anointing Oil,
17. Inscence,
18. The Sabbath,
19. Skilled Craftsmen to make all the above items.

Exodus Chapter 25 says the Lord said to Moses on Mount Sinai, "Tell the Israelites to bring offerings for the Tabernacle and Ark and receive them from each man, whose heart prompts him to give. The offerings you have to receive from the Israelites are: gold, silver, bronze, blue, purple, and scarlet yarn and fine linen, goat hair, ram skins dyed red, and hides of sea cows, acacia wood, olive oil for the light, spices for the anointing oil and fragrant incense and onyx stones and other gems to be mounted on the ephod and breastpiece. Then, have them make a sanctuary for me, and I will dwell among them. Make this tabernacle and all its furnishings exactly like the pattern I will show you."

1. Lord's Description of the Ark

"Let them make a chest of acacia wood – two and half cubits long, a cubit and a half wide, and a cubit and a half high (This is about 1.1 meters long, 0.7 meters wide and 0.7 meters high). Overlay, it with pure gold, both inside and outside and make a gold molding around it. Cast four gold rings for it and fasten them to its four feet, with two rings on one side and two rings on the other. Then, make poles of acacia wood and overlay them with gold. Insert the poles into the rings on the sides of the chest to carry it. The poles are to remain in the rings of this Ark, they are not to be removed. Then, put in the ark, the testimony, which I will give you."

"Make an atonement cover of pure gold- two and half cubits long and a cubit and a half wide (This is about 1.1 meters long and 0.7 meters wide). And make two cherubim, out of hammered gold at the ends of the cover of the chest. Make one cherub sit on one end and the other cherub on the other end of the cover. Thus, two cherubim on either side of the cover. The cherubim are to have their wings spread upward, overshadowing the cover with them. The cherubim are to face each other, looking towards the cover. Place the cover on top of the Ark and put in the Ark, the Testimony, which I will give you. There, above the cover between the two cherubim that are over the Ark of the Testimony, I will meet with you and give you all my commands for the Israelites."

2. Lord's description of the Table

The Lord said, "Make a table of acacia wood – two cubits long, a cubit wide and a cubit and half high (This is 0.9 meters long, 0.5 meters wide and 0.7 meters high). Overlay it with pure gold and make a gold molding around it. Also make around it a rim of a hand breadth (about 8 centimeters) wide and put a gold molding on the rim. Make four gold rings for the table and fasten them to the four corners, where the four legs are. The rings are to be close to the rim to hold the poles used to carry the table. Make the poles of acacia wood, overlay them with gold and carry the table with them. Make its plates and dishes of pure gold, as well as its pitchers and bowls for the pouring out of offerings. Put the bread of the Presence on this table to be before me at all times."

3. *Lord's Description of the Lampstand*

The Lord said, "Make a lamp stand of pure gold and hammer it out, base and shaft; its flower like cups, buds and blossoms shall be of one piece with it. Six branches are to extend from the sides of the lamp stand – three on one side and three on the other. Three cups shaped like almond flowers with buds and blossoms are to be on one branch, three on to the next branch, and the same for all the six branches extending from the lamp stand. And on the lamp stand, there are to be four cups shaped like almond flower with buds and blossoms. One bud shall be under the first pair of branches extending from the lamp stand, a second bud under the second pair, and the third bud under the third pair – six branches in all. The buds and branches shall all be of one piece with the lampstand, hammered out of pure gold"

"Then make its seven lamps and set them up on it so that, they light the space in front of it. Its wick trimmers and trays are to be of pure gold. A talent (about 34 kilograms) of pure gold is to be used for the lampstand and all these accessories. See that you make them according to the pattern shown to you on the mountain."

4. *Lord's Description of the Tabernacle*

The Lord said to Moses, "Make the tabernacle (Tent) with ten curtains of finely twisted linen and blue, purple and scarlet yarn, with cherubim worked into them by skilled craftsman. All the curtains are to be of the same size – twenty eight cubits long and four cubits wide (This is about 12.5 meters long and 1.8 meters wide). Join five of the curtains together and do the same with the other five. Make loops of blue material along the edge of the end curtain in one set, and do the same with the end curtain of the other set. Make fifty loops on one curtain and fifty loops on the end curtain of the other set, with the loops opposite to each other. Then, make fifty gold clasps and use them to fasten the curtains together so that, the tabernacle is a unit."

The Lord also said, "Make curtains of goat hair for the tent over the tabernacle – eleven together. All eleven curtains are to be the same size – thirty cubits long and four cubits wide (That is about 13.5 meters long and 1.8 meters wide). Join five of these curtains together into one set and the other six into another set. Fold the six curtains double at the front of the tent. Make fifty loops along the edge of the end curtain in one set and along the edge of the end curtain in the other set. Then, make fifty bronze clasps and put them in the loops to fasten the tent together as a unit. As for the additional length of the tent curtains, the half curtain that is left over is to hang down at the rear of the tabernacle. The tent curtains will be a cubit longer on both sides; what is left will hang over the sides of the tabernacle so as to cover it. Make for the tent a covering of ram skins dyed red and over that a covering of hides of sea cows."

"Make upright frames of acacia wood for the tabernacle. Each frame is to be ten cubits long and a cubit and half wide (That is about 4.5 meters long and 0.7 meters wide) with two projections set parallel to each other. Make all the frames of the tabernacle in this way. Make twenty frames for the south side of the tabernacle and make forty silver bases to go under them - two bases for each frame, one under each projection. For the other side, the north side of the tabernacle make twenty frames and forty silver bases – two under each frame. Make six frames for the far end, that is, the west end of the tabernacle, and make two frames for the corners at the far end. At these two corners, they must be double from the bottom all the way to the top, and fitted into a single ring; both shall be like that. So, there will be eight frames and sixteen silver bases- two under each frame."

The Lord further said, "Make cross bars of acacia wood: five for the frames on one side of the tabernacle, five for those on the other side, and five for the frames on the west, at the end of the tabernacle. The center cross bar is to extend from end to end at the middle of the frames. Overlay the frames with gold and make gold rings to hold the crossbars. Also, overlay the crossbars with gold."

Further, God said, "Set up the tabernacle according to the plan shown to you on Mount Sinai. Make a curtain of blue, purple and scarlet yarn and finely twisted linen, with cherubim worked into it by a skilled craftsman. Hang it with gold hooks on four posts of acacia wood overlaid with gold and standing on four silver bases. Hang the curtain from the clasps and place the Ark of Testimony behind the curtain. The curtain will separate the Holy Place from the Most Holy Place. Put the atonement cover on the Ark of the Testimony in the Most Holy Place. Place the table outside the curtain on the north side of the tabernacle and put the lamp stand opposite it on the south side. From the entrance to the tent, make a curtain of blue, purple and scarlet yarn and finely twisted linen – the work of an embroiderer. Make gold hooks for the curtain and five posts of acacia wood over laid with gold and cast five bronze bases for them."

5. Lord's Description of the Altar for Burnt Offering

The Lord said to Moses, "Build an altar of acacia wood three cubits high: it is to be square, five cubits long and five cubits wide (That is about 2.3 meters long and 2.3 meters wide and 1.4 meters high). Make a horn at each of the four corners, so that the horns and the altar are of one piece, and overlay the altar with bronze. Make all its utensils of bronze – its pots to remove the ashes, and its shovels, sprinkling bowls, meat forks, and fire pans. Make a grating for it, a bronze network, and make a bronze ring at each of the four corners of the network. Put it under the ledge of the altar, so that it is half way up the altar. Make poles of acacia wood for the altar and overlay them with bronze. The poles are to be inserted into the rings, so they will be on two sides of the altar, when it is carried. Make the altar hollow, out of boards. It is to be made just as you were shown on Mount Sinai."

6. *Lord's Description of the Courtyard*

The Lord said to Moses, "Make a courtyard for the tabernacle. The south side of the courtyard shall be a hundred cubits long (about 46 meters) and is to have curtains of finely twisted linen, with twenty posts and twenty bronze bases and with silver hooks and bands on the posts. The north side of the courtyard shall also be a hundred cubits (that is about 46 meters) long and is to have curtains, with twenty posts and twenty brass bases and with silver hooks and bands on the posts. The west end of the courtyard shall be fifty cubits (that is about 23 meters) wide and have curtains, with ten posts and ten bases. On the east end of the courtyard, towards the sunshine, shall also be fifty cubits (that is about 23 meters) wide. Curtains of fifteen cubits (that is about 6.9 meters) long are to be on one side of the entrance, with three posts and three bases, and curtains fifteen cubits (that is about 6.9 meters) long are to be on the other side, with three posts and three bases. For the entrance of the courtyard, provide a curtain twenty cubits (that is about 9 meters) long, of blue, purple, and scarlet yarn and finely twisted linen – the work of an embroiderer – with four posts and four bases. All the posts around the courtyard are to have silver bands and hooks, and bronze bases. The courtyard shall be a hundred cubits long and fifty cubits wide (that is about 46 meters long and 23 meters wide) with curtains of finely twisted linen five cubits (that is about 2.3 meters) high and with bronze bases. All the other articles used in the service of the tabernacle, whatever their function, including all the tent pegs for it and those for the courtyard are to be of bronze."

7. *Lord's Description of the Altar of Incense*

The Lord said to Moses, "Make an altar of acacia wood for burning incense. It is to be a square, a cubit long and a cubit wide and two cubits high (that is about 0.5 meters long, 0.5 meters wide and 0.9 meters high) – its horns of one piece with it. Overlay the top and all its sides and the horns with pure gold and make gold molding around it. Make two gold rings for the altar below the molding – two on opposite sides – to hold the poles used to carry it. Make the poles of acacia wood and overlay them with gold. Put the altar in front of the curtain that is before the Ark of Testimony before the atonement cover that is over the Testimony – where I will meet with you."

The Lord also said, "Aaron must burn the fragrant incense on the altar every morning when he tends the lamps. He must burn incense again when he lights the lamps at twilight, so incense will burn regularly before the Lord for generations to come. Do not offer on this altar any other incense or any burnt offering or grain offering and do not pour a drink offering on it. Once a year, Aaron shall make atonement on its horns. This annual atonement must be made with the blood of the atoning sin offering for the generations to come. It is most holy to the Lord."

8. to 12. *Lord's Description of other requirement of the Ark of Testimony and Tabernacle*

The Lord discussed with Moses on Mount Sinai, the requirement of the tabernacle, such as; i) Oil for the lamps, ii) The priestly garments, iii) The Ephod, iv) The Breast piece,

v) Priestly garments, vi) Consecration of priests, vii) Atonement money, viii) Basin for washing, ix) Anointing oil, x) incense, xi) The Sabbath, and xii) Skilled craftsman to make the tabernacle, Ark of Testimony and others.

Readers are advised to go through Chapters 25 to 30 of the book of Exodus in the Old Testament, to know all minute details of the above.

According to Exodus Chapter 31:18, when the Lord finished speaking to Moses on Mount Sinai, he gave Moses the two tablets of the Testimony, the tablets of stone inscribed by the finger of God.

But, when Moses came down from Mount Sinai after forty days, the Israelites made a golden calf and were worshipping it as their God. Moses was furious to see this and threw the Stone tablets of the Ten Commandments on the ground, when they broke into pieces. Then, according to the Lord's commandment, Moses chiseled out two new stone tables and took them to Mount Sinai again. Moses was with the Lord for forty days and forty nights without eating bread or drinking water, and he wrote on the tables the words of the covenant – The Ten Commandments (Exodus 34:28).

Moses came down from Mount Sinai with the two stone tablets of Ten Commandment and his face shone, because he had spoken with the Lord this made the Israelites afraid to come near Moses. Then Moses called them all and explained what the Lord told him, the building of the tabernacle and Lord's selection of Bezalel and Oholiab who had the gift of making the Ark and all other items of gold, silver, bronze, curtains, etc. All of them started making the Tabernacle, Ark, Table, Lamp stand, Altar of Incense, Altar of Burnt Offering, Basin for washing, The Ephod, Breast piece, etc. exactly according to what the Lord told Moses on Mount Sinai. Moses supervised all these activities to ensure that the Lord's commandments are followed exactly in the making of all these.

Thus, Moses finished the work entrusted to him by the Lord on Mount Sinai.

Then, the cloud covered the tent of meeting and the glory of the Lord filled the tabernacle. Moses could not enter the Tent of Meeting, because the cloud had settled upon it, and the glory of the Lord filled the tabernacle.

In all the travels of the Israelites, whenever, the cloud lifted from above the tabernacle, they would set out; but if the cloud did not lift, they did not set out; until the day it lifted. So, the cloud of the Lord was over the tabernacle by day, and fire was in the cloud by night, in the sight of all the house of Israel during all their travels.

The following picture shows the outer tent of the tabernacle, the courtyard, location of altar of burnt offering, Laver, table of presence bread, Altar of incense, and Ark of Testimony in the Most Holy Place and the Holy Place, etc.

Outer Tent (See below for enlarged view of inner structure)

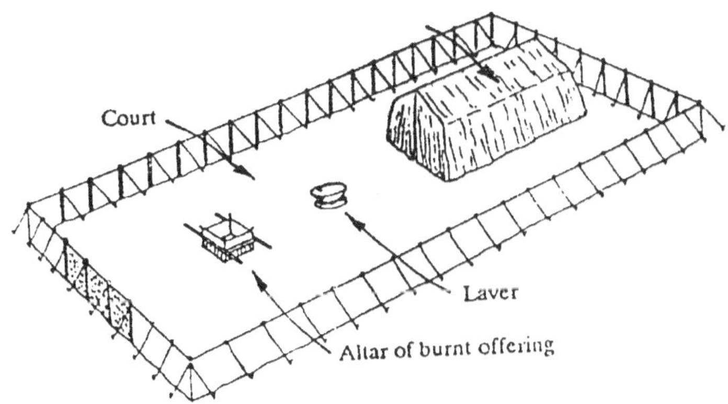

ABOVE: THE TABERNACLE AND ITS COURT

ENLARGED CUTAWAY OF INNER STRUCTURE

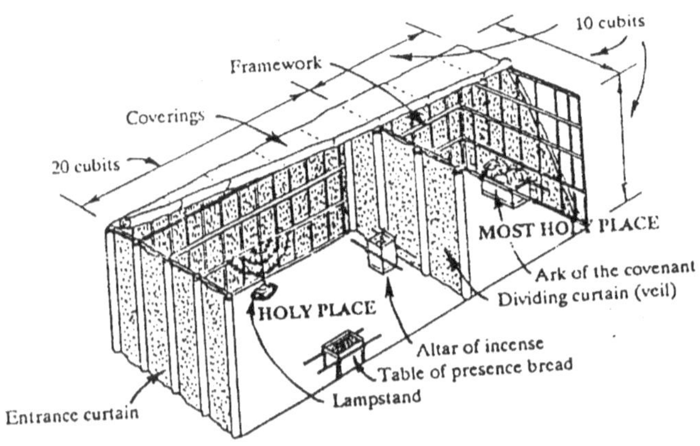

THE TABERNACLE

(Ark of Testimony is shown on the inside back cover of this book)

When the Israelites left Egypt from the bondage of King Pharoah and traveled through deserts before reaching the "Promised Land" of Canaan, God gave detailed arrangements for their organized religious life. According to these arrangements, the place of worship of all Israelites is a Tabernacle or tent set up in the center of their camp. This Tabernacle was the symbol of God's presence and a sign that God dwelt among his people. It was known as the "Tent of Meeting" (Exodus 39:32), as it was the place, where God met his people. It was also known as "Tent of Testimony" (Exodus 38:21) to remind the people that within it, in the Ark, was the testimony of God, the law which was to guide and control their lives.

The entire Tabernacle is easily portable from place to place, wherever Israelites traveled in reaching Canaan from Egypt. The Tabernacle mainly consisted of a two – roomed structure under a tent. The front room was called the "The Holy Place", with three articles in it. Against one wall was a table of acacia wood laid with gold and on it were twelve cakes of "Presence Bread" in two rows of six in each row to represent the twelve tribes of Israelites and a cup of wine, in symbolic acknowledgement that Israelites lived always in the presence of God. These twelve cakes were renewed on each Sabbath day (Exodus 25:23 to 30 and Lev. 24:5 to 9). Against the opposite wall was a seven branched ornamented lamp stand, made entirely of gold (Exodus 25:31 to 40; 26:35). Against the dividing curtain (Veil) was an altar used solely for burning incense.

The room behind the veil was called the "Most Holy Place." The only piece of furniture in this room was the "Ark of Covenant", or "Ark of Testimony", or "Covenant Box" (Exodus 25:10 to 16 and 26:34). Its richly ornamented lid of the wooden box was called the "Mercy Seat", which was the throne of the invisible God. The symbolic guardians of this throne were two Golden Cherubims (Exodus 25:17 to 21 and I Samuel 4:4). Inside the Ark were placed the two stone tables of Ten Commandments (Deut. 10:1 to 5). But, Hebrews 9:4 says that the Ark contained a gold jar of Manna, Aaron's staff that had budded, and the two tables of stone with Ten Commandments.

Only the priests could enter the Holy Place (Numbers 18:1-7 and Heb. 9:6). Only the High Priest could enter the Most Holy Place once in a year on the day of Atonement (Lev. 16: 11-15 and Heb. 9:7).

Movement of the Tabernacle with Its Ark

Whenever the Israelites moved from one place to the other, after Mount Sinai, where they assembled the Tabernacle they used to cover the Ark with a cloth and the Levites (priests) carried the Ark on their shoulders with the poles fixed to the Ark. The Ark usually went in front of the main procession of Israelites (Numbers 4:5 and 6; 10:33).

When the Israelites crossed the river Jordan to enter the Promised Land, the Levites carrying the Ark entered the water of river Jordan, when the water got separated leaving a dry land for the Israelites to cross and the Levites carrying the Ark stood in the river bed till all the Israelites crossed the river on dry land (Joshua 3:11-17).

For the first battle in Canaan, God directed the priests to take the Ark from the tabernacle and carry it around the city of Jericho, once every day. On the seventh day, they shouted seven times and the walls of Jericho collapsed and was conquered by the Israelites (Josh 6:1-5).

Several generations later, Israelites again carried the Ark into a battle against Philistines. But, the Israelites had done so not by the direction of God. So, Israelites were defeated by Philistines and the Ark was taken away by Philistines (I Sam. 4:3 and 4, 11).

But, the Philistines suffered many plagues by keeping the Ark by the side of their God Dagon. They had to transfer it from place to place, from Ashod to Gath then to Ekron to avoid the curse of God and after seven months, the Philistines returned the Ark to Israelites (I Sam 5:1-12, 6:1-16).

For the next twenty years, the Ark remained in the country house in Kiriath – Jearim (I Sam 6:21 and 7:2).

When King David was the King of Jerusalem, he decided to bring back the Ark to make Jerusalem, a center of religion of the Nation. But David did not follow the exact manner of the Ark being carried by Levites on their shoulders. But, he placed the Ark on a cart driven by oxen and as the oxen stumbled, Uzzah who was driving the cart touched the Ark to arrest it from falling down and God smote him for this error of touching and he died (II Sam 6:2-10).

Three months later, after King David realized his mistake of carrying the Ark on a cart instead of Levite priests carrying it on their shoulders, he arranged Levite priests to carry the Ark to Jerusalem (II Sam 6:12 and 13 and I Chr. 15:13-15). King

David danced before the Ark when it was brought into Jerusalem and placed it in a tent specially prepared for it (II Sam 6:12 and 13, I Chr. 15:13–15).

Later on, when King Solomon, son of King David constructed the temple in Jerusalem, he placed the Ark in the Most Holy Place (I Kings 8:6-11). Apparently, the Ark was removed during the regime of the wicked Manasseh. But, Josiah restored it to its original place (II Chr. 35:1-3).

In the year 587 B.C., King Nebuchadnezzar of Babylon raided Jerusalem and plundered all valuables of the temple and took them to Babylon and placed them in the temples of their Gods (II King 24:13). The Ark was also taken to Babylon. Thereafter, there is no proper record of the Ark but probably King Cyprus of Persia who rebuilt the temple in Jerusalem might have brought the Ark back to Jerusalem (II King 24:13).

The two cherubim sitting on the cover of the Ark depicts winged creatures of some heavenly angelic order. Cherubim usually acted as guardians for the Almighty and his interests.

When Adam rebelled against God in the Eden Garden, God sent cherubim to guard the Tree of Life (Gen 3:24). In the tabernacle of Israelites, two cherubim were placed on the lid of the Ark. The lid was known as the "Mercy Seat" the throne of God and the cherubim were the guardians of the throne (Exo 25 :18-22, I Sam 4:4, II Sam 6:2, and II Kings 19:15, Psalms 80:1, Heb 9:5).

In the magnificent temple constructed by King Solomon in Jerusalem the Most Holy place had two huge cherubim stretching from wall to wall (I King 6:23-28).

In the vision of Ezekiel, cherubim supported the chariot throne of God (Ezek 1:4-28; 10:1-22, Psalms 18:10).

Cherubim were pictured on the coverings and curtains of the tablernacle (Exo 26: 1 and 31), the walls of the temple (IKings 6:29, Ezek 41: 17-20 and 25) and on the mobile lavers that belonged to the temple (IKings 7:29 and 36)

12.

Ten Commandments of the Lord Handed Over to Moses on Mount Sinai

Israelites were in slavery for four hundred thirty six years in Egypt under King Pharaoh and had undergone many troubles. God wanted to take them to the land of Cannan, known as the "promised Land" where honey and milk flowed. God selected Moses to meet the Pharaoh and plead with him to release the Israelites, saying "Let my people go." As Moses accepted to God that he was slow in speech and of a low tongue, God said that he would be with him always and teach him what he would say to the Pharaoh. God said that Aaron, the Levite and brother of Moses will help Moses to speak what God commanded (Exodus 4:10 to 16).

After meeting the Pharaoh along with Aaron, Moses pleaded for release of Israelites. God punished the Egyptians by sending ten deadly curses. At last, king Pharaoh allowed the Israelites to leave Egypt under the leadership of Moses. Israelites journeyed from Rameses to Succoth and there were six lakh men besides children. When they approached the sea they saw the Egyptians chasing them from behind. God told Moses to stretch his hand over the sea, and Moses did so; and the water of the sea were divided and Israelites crossed the sea on dry land. When the Egyptians entered the midst of sea,

Moses again stretched out his hand over the sea, and the water joined, and all the Egyptians perished (Exodus 14:16 to 28).

According to Exodus 19:1 to 3, in the third month after leaving Egypt, the Israelites camped before Mount Sinai. Moses went up the mountain unto God and Moses was told many things by God, which he passed on to the Israelites. The Lord said to Moses, come up to me into the mount, and be there: and I will give thee two tablets of stone, and a law and commandments which I have written: that thou mayest teach them.

The Ten Commandments were written by God himself on the two stone tablets on both the sides. Moses came down from Mount Sinai carrying the two stone tablets with the Ten Commandments.

The Ten Commandment of God, in simple language are as follows:-

1. I am the Lord thy God, and thou shall have no other God except me,

2. Thou shall not worship any image,

3. Thou shall not take the name of the Lord lightly and in vain.

4. Thou shall keep the Sabbath Day as Holy.

5. Thou shall honour your father and mother, so that your days on the land may be long.

6. Thou shall not kill.

7. Thou shall not commit adultery,

8. Thou shall not steal.

9. Thou shall not bear false witness against thy neighbour,

10. Thou shall not covet anything of your neighbour.

(Exodus 20: 1 to 17).

According to Exodus 32: 17 to 20, when Moses and Joshua came down from Mount Sinai, they heard noise of the Israelites, as they were dancing. They saw a golden calf and all were dancing before it. Moses' anger waxed hot and he cast the tablets out of his hands and broke them beneath Mountain Sinai. Moses took the golden calf, burnt it in fire, ground it to powder, mixed it with water and made all the Israelites drink it.

Then God asked Moses to make two tablets of stone like the first ones and he will write upon these tablets the words that were in the first tablets which were broken by Moses (Exodus 34:1 to 6).

Moses did accordingly and went up to Mount Sinai. Moses was there with the Lord for forty days and forty nights without bread or water. And he wrote upon the tablets the words of the convenant, the Ten Commandments. Moses came down the mountain with two tablets of stone with the Ten Commandments written again and met Aaron and all Israelites. As Moses had seen with a veil. God, his face show, and he had to cover his face. Moses gave the Ten Commandments to them and told all things which he heard from the Lord (Exodus 34:27 to 35).

13.

Observation of Sabbath Day

For the first time, this term "Sabbath" was used by Lord Jehovah, when he was speaking to Moses on Mount Sinai (Exodus 20:8). God said to Moses, "Remember the Sabbath day to keep it holy."

The exact language, which was in use in those ancient days is not very well known, but this term " Sabbath" is still used as such in all countries, even though these countries use different languages. Till now, this term has not been translated into any other language in any country and it remains as such.

This term "Sabbath" appears even in the book of Genesis 2:1 to 3, which says, "Thus, the heavens and earth were finished and all the host of them. And on the seventh day God ended from all his work, which he made and he rested on the seventh day from all his work. And God blessed the seventh day and sanctified it."

According to Exodus 16; 4 to 28, when the Israelites murmured in the wilderness of sin (Which is between Elim and Sinai) for food, God said to Moses that he would rain bread from heaven (Manna), which they can collect every day for six days to meet their requirement and on the seventh day, there would be no bread falling from heaven. So, they should collect twice the daily quantity on the sixth day itself. Moses conveyed this message of the Lord to all Israelites. Some Isrealites went on the seventh day (The Sabbath day) also to collect manna, but they found none. Thus even manna bread from heaven was stopped by God on the Sabbath day.

According to Exodus 20:8 to 11, when Moses met the Lord on Mount Sinai after the Lord spoke to Moses about the Ten Commandments, the Lord said, "Remember the Sabbath day to keep it holy. Six days, thou shalt labour and do all thy work. But the seventh day is the Sabbath of the Lord thy God: in it, thou shall not do any work, thou nor thy son nor thy daughter, nor thy servant, nor stranger that is within thy gates: for in six days the Lord made heaven and earth, the sea and all that in them is and rested the seventh day: wherefore, the Lord blessed the sabbath day and hallowed it."

Exodus 31:12 to 18 says the Lord spake unto Moses, saying, "speak thou also unto the children of Israel," saying, "verily my Sabbaths ye shall keep: for it is a sign between me and you throughout your generations that ye may know that I am the Lord that doth sanctify you. ye shall keep the Sabbath therefore: for it is holy unto you, everyone that defileth it for whosever doeth any work therein, that soul shall be cut off from among his people. Six days may work be done, but the seventh day is the Sabbath of the rest, holy to the Lord: whosoever doeth any work on the Sabbath day, he shall surely be put to death. Wherefore the children of Israel shall keep the Sabbath to observe the Sabbath throughout their generations for a perpetual covenant. It is a sign between me and the children of Israel forever: for in six days the Lord made heaven and earth and on the seventh day, he rested and was refreshed.

Again, according to Exodus 35:1 to 3, Moses came down from Mount Sinai, gathered all Israelites and told them, "These are the words which the Lord hath commanded that ye should do them –six days shall work be done, but on the seventh day there shall be to you a holy day, a Sabbath of rest to the Lord: Whosoever doeth work therein shall be put to death. Ye shall kindle no fire throughout your habitations upon the Sabbath Day."

Thus, the Lord was very strict with all Israelites to observe the Sabbath day as a day of complete rest.

The Lord spoke to prophet Ezekiel (Ezek 20:12 and 13 and 16 and 24,22:8 and 26), saying, "Moreover, I gave them my Sabbath to be a sign between me and them that they might know that I am the Lord that sactify them. But the house of Israel rebelled against me in the wilderness: my Sabbaths they greatly polluted, for their heart went after their idols. He would pour out his fury upon them to accomplish his anger against them in the wilderness."

Ezekiel 22:8 and 26 says that the Lord said, "Thou hast despised mine holy things and hast profaned my Sabbaths. The priests have violated the law of the lord and have hid their eyes from Sabbath. Therefore I will pour out my indignation upon them."

Prophet Nehemiah said (Nene 13:15 to 22), "I saw in Judah some treading wine presses on the Sabbath and bringing in sheaves, wine, grapes etc., on asses to Jerusalem on the Sabbath day and I testified against them. People of Tyre also were selling fish on Sabbath day. I told them that it was evil to profane Sabbath day. You will bring more wraths upon Israel by profaning Sabbath. I ordered that the gates of Jerusalem should be closed on Sabbath days and warned all merchants not to come on Sabbath days."

The Lord said to prophet Jeremiah (Jer 17:19to 27), "Go and stand in the gate of the children of the people, where by all kings of Judah enter and go out and tell them not to bear any burden on the Sabbath day into Jerusalem neither do ye work, but hallow the Sabbath as the Lord commanded to their father also. If they don't obey, then I will kindle a fire the gates in thereof and it shall devour the palaces of Jerusalem and the fire shall not quenched."

MENTION OF SABBATH DAY IN THE FOUR GOSPELS

In the four gospels of the New Testament also there are atleast five references about the Sabbath Day. They are briefly explained below:-

1. Disciples eating corn on Sabbath day –According to Matthew 12:1 to 8, Mark 2:23 to 28 and Luke 6:1 to 10, Jesus went on a Sabbath day through the corn fields and his disciples were a hungered lot and began to pluck the ears of corn and eat. But when the Pharisees saw it, they said to Jesus, "Behold, thy disciples do that which is not lawful to do upon the Sabbath day." But, Jesus said to them, "Have ye not read what David did, when he was hungered and they that were with him.? How he entered into the house of God and did eat the shew bread, which was not lawful for him to eat, neither for them, which were with him, but only for the priests? Or have ye not read in the law how that on the Sabbath days the priest in the temple profane the Sabbath and are blameless ? But I say unto you, that in this place is greater than the temple. For the son of Man is lord even of the Sabbath day. In Mark 2:27, Jesus said to the Pharisees that the Sabbath was made for man and not man for the Sabbath.

2. On a Sabbath day, Jesus healed a man with a withered hand. According to Matthew 12: 9 to 14, Mark 3: 1 to 6 and Luke 6: 6 to 11, Jesus went into a synagogue on a Sabbath day. There was a man who had his hand withered. The scribes and Pharisees watched him, whether he would heal on the Sabbath day, that they might find an accusation against him. Jesus knew their

thoughts and asked the man which had the withered hand to stand in midst of all. Then Jesus asked him", Is it lawful on Sabbath days to do good or to do evil? To save life or to destroy it? "Looking around about all of them, Jesus asked him to stretch forth his hand, and he did so, and it was restored whole as the other hand. All of them were filled with madness and communed with one another as to what they might do to Jesus.

3. On a Sabbath day, Jesus healed a woman who had a spirit of infirmity for eighteen years – According to John 13:10 to 17 Jesus was teaching in one of the synagogues on a Sabbath day. There was a woman, who had spirit of infirmity for eighteen years and was bowed down and couldn't lift up herself. Jesus saw her and laid his hands on her, and said, "Women, thou art loosed from thine infirmity." She was cured immediately and glorified God. The rulers of the synagogue were filled with indignation, because Jesus had healed her on a Sabbath day. But, Jesus said, "thou hypocrite, doth not each one of you on the Sabbath day loose his Ox or his ass from the stall and lead it away to watering ? This woman, daughter of Abraham was bound by satan for eighteen years, and can she be not loosed from this bondage on a Sabbath day?" The adversaries of Jesus were ashamed and all the people rejoiced for all the glorious things that were done by Jesus.

4. Jesus healed on a Sabbath day, a man having infirmity for thirty eight years at the pool of Bethesda –According to John 5: 2 to 11, Jesus came to Jerusalem where, by the side of the sheep market, there was a pool, which is called Bethesada, having five porches. In these lay a great multitude of impotent folk of blind, halt, withered etc., waiting for moving of water by an angel. At a certain season an angel went down and moved the

water in the pool, and whosoever first stepped into the water was made whole of whatsoever disease he had. A certain man was there, who had a infirmity for thirty eight years. When Jesus saw him and knew that he was waiting there for thirty eight years, Jesus told him," will thou be made whole? "The man answered Jesus by saying, "Sir, I have no man to put me into the water, when it is troubled by the angel. While I am coming, another steppeth down before me, "Jesus said to him "Rise, take up thy bed and walk." Immediately he was made whole he and walked away. The same day was a Sabbath day. The Jews said to the man, "It is a Sabbath day and it is not lawful for thee to carry thy bed and walk." The man told them that he who made him whole, asked him to take up the bed and walk. Later on, he told them that it was Jesus who made him whole. The Jews sought to slay Jesus, because he had done these things on the Sabbath day.

5. Jesus healed on a Sabbath day a man who was blind from his birth -According to John 9: 1 to 28 as Jesus passed by, he saw a man, who was blind from his birth. The disciples asked Jesus, saying, "Master who did sin? This man or his parents, that he was born blind?" Jesus said, "Neither hath this man sinned nor his parents: but that the works of God should be made manifested in him." Jesus anointed his eyes with clay, and said to him, "Go, wash in the pool of Siloam" (which is by interpretation, sent). The man washed in pool of Siloam and received his sight. The Pharisees said that Jesus was not a man of God.

14.

Crucification of Jesus Christ, Seven Words Spoken by Jesus from the Cross, Resurrection and Ascension into Heaven

In the present days, in almost all countries the severest punishment given by the court of justice to a person who had committed a serious crime is hanging to death with rope. But as this kind of punishment is considered as cruel in some countries, hanging had been abolished and killing by an electric shock had been introduced.

Published literature shows that in the early years, the severest punishment to a criminal was crucifixion. Such punishment was first introduced by Persians (now Iranians), nearly four hundred years before Jesus Christ was crucified. Later on, the Roman emperors introduced crucifiction as capital punishment for criminals like, murderers, robbers, rude slaves etc. The Roman emperor Constantine, who was ruling in the 4th century (320A.D. to 326 A.D) abolished crucifiction when he was converted as a Christian, as he was moved with the cruel death of Jesus Christ on the cross. Later on, he was responsible for construction of many churches in Bethlehem, Jerusalem and many parts of Israel. The capital punishment given by Jews was stoning to death. Stephen was stoned to death. The usual procedure followed for crucification was that the criminal was beaten by the soldiers and then forced to carry a heavy cross made with raw wood on his shoulders to the place of crucification. There, the cross was placed on ground, and the criminal was made to stretch himself on the cross with his hands stretched out on the cross bar. A wooden support was fixed at the legs so that the criminal did not slip from the cross. Then the most cruel part of crucifiction was to drive big metal nails, making use of big hammers, into the two hands and legs, when the criminals used to cry out of pain and blood gushing out. Then, with the help of ropes tied to the cross, it was raised up and the criminal was hung on the cross with severe pain. In order to reduce the pain the Roman soldiers gave wine mixed with vinegar to drink. A playcard was fixed at the top of the cross showing the name of the criminal. Profuse bleeding, made the criminal die. But, some times, in order to hasten the death, the soldiers broke the legs of the criminal with a sword, thus causing more bleeding which hastens death quickly. After the criminal was dead on the cross, the dead body was handed over to the relatives for burial. Crucification was usually carried out in prominent places outside the city, so that many people may see it and avoid committing any serious crime.

In Jesus' days Caesar Augustus was the emperor of Roman world and Quirinius was the Governor of Syria. Herod was Tetrarch of Galilee (Luke 1:5). Annas, the father-in-law of Caiaphas, who was the High Priest at that time was also in Jerusalem. Pontius Pilot was the Roman Governor in Judea (Luke 3: 1 and 2).

According to Luke 2: 41 to 52 every year, the parents of Jesus were going from Nazareth to Jerusalem (131 kms) for the feast of the Passover. When Jesus was twelve years old, according to their custom, Jesus' parents went to Jerusalem, taking with them Jesus also. After the feast was over, while his parents were returning home, boy Jesus stayed behind in Jerusalem. But, the parents did not realise it and thought that

Jesus might be with a group of people returning to Nazareth. After three days journey, the parents knew that Jesus was not returning with them to Nazareth and they went back to Jerusalem in search of Jesus. When they came to Jerusalem, they found Jesus in the temple courts sitting amongst the teachers, listening to them and asking them questions. Everyone who heard Jesus was amazed at his understanding and his answers? Then, Jesus went back to Nazareth with his parents and grew up there and was obedient to his parents. Jesus grew up in wisdom and stature and in favour with God and men. Thus Jesus Christ being the son of God was very clever from the age of twelve itself.

Jesus was baptized by John the Baptist in river Jordan, when Jesus was thirty years old. As Jesus came out of water of the river Jordan, the heaven was opened and Holy Spirit descended on him in the form of a dove and a voice came from heaven, saying, "You are my son whom I love :With you I am well pleased" (Luke 3: 21 to 23).

Immediately after baptism, Jesus was led by the spirit in to a desert, where Jesus fasted for forty days and forty nights praying. After that, Jesus was tempted thrice by Satan, but Jesus conquered Satan. Jesus drove away the Satan. Jesus was filled with the power of the Holy Spirit and returned from the desert to Galilee and taught in their synagogues and everyone praised him. News about Jesus was spread in the whole countryside. Jesus selected his disciples near the Sea of Galilee. Then, Jesus went to Nazareth, where he had been brought up and preached in the synagogue. The people in Nazareth were amazed at the gracious words that came from the lips of Jesus and said, "Is he not the son of Joseph?" Jesus said that, "No prophet is accepted in his home town." All the people in the synagogue of Nazareth were furious with that Jesus spoke and they got up, drove him out of the town. Then, Jesus went to Galilee (Capernaum) teaching in the synagogues, preaching the good news of the kingdom and healing every diseases and sickness among people. News about him spread all over Syria and people brought to him all who were ill with various diseases, those suffering from severe pain, the demon-possessed, those having seizures, and the paralyzed and he healed them all. Large crowds of people from Galilee, the Decapolis, Jerusalem, Judea and regions across the Jordan also followed Jesus (Matthew 4:1to 25 Mark 1:12 and 13, Luke 4:1 to 28). Jesus Christ had Heavenly power to raise the dead. He raised Lazarus, the brother of Mary and Martha at Bethany, who was dead. According to John 11:45 to 53, when Jesus Christ made Lazarus rise from the dead at Bethany, many Jews who saw this miracle believed on Jesus. But, some of them went to the Pharisees and told them what things Jesus had done. Then, the chief priest and Pharisees gathered to consider what they should do to Jesus who was performing many miracles. They all felt that if Jesus was performing many miracles, all men will believe him: and the Romans shall come and take away both their place and the nation. Caiaphas, the high priest said that Jesus should die for that nation. From that day onwards, they took counsel together for to put Jesus to death. Jesus Christ predicted his death.

As Jesus Christ was the Son of God, he could predict his death and mentioned to his disciples many times, but they could not understand Jesus' words properly.

According to Matthew 16:13 to 23, when Jesus came into the coasts of Caesarea, Philippi asked his disciples, saying, "whom do men say that I the Son of man am? Simon Peter said "Thou art the Christ, the Son of the living God, "Jesus asked his disciples not to tell anyone that he was the Christ. From that time onwards, Jesus began to explain to his disciples that he must go to Jerusalem and suffer many things at the hands of the elders, chief priests and teachers of the law and that he must be killed and on the third day be raised to life. Peter took Jesus aside and began to rebuke him, saying, "Never, Lord, this shall never happen to you." Jesus turned, and said to Peter, "Get behind me, you do not have in mind the things of God, but the things of men."

Similarly, after transfiguration of Jesus on the mountain (Matthew 17: 1 to 9), as Jesus was coming down with his three disciples, Peter, James and John, Jesus instructed them, "Do no tell anyone what you have seen, until the Son of Man has been raised from the dead."

According to Matthew 20: 17 to 19, Jesus going up to Jerusalem took the twelve disciples apart in the way, and said unto them, "Behold, we go to Jerusalem: and the Son of Man shall be betrayed unto the chief priest and unto the scribes and they shall condemn him to death. And shall deliver him to the Gentiles to mock, and scourge and to crucify him: and the third day he shall rise again."

Matthew 26:2 also says that after Jesus spoke to the multitudes, he said to his disciples, "Ye know that after two days is the feast of the Passover, and the Son of Man is betrayed to be crucified."

All these instances are repeated in Mark 8:31-33: 9:9 and 10:32: to 34; 14:3 to 9 and Luke 18:31 to 33; and John 12: 20 to 36.

Last Journey of Jesus to Jerusalem

According to Mark 10 :32 to 33 on the way to Jerusalem Jesus told his disciples what things would happen at Jerusalem saying, "Behold, we go up to Jerusalem and the Son of man shall be delivered unto the chief priests and they shall condemn him to death but, he will rise on the third day."

According to Mathew 21: 1 to 10, when Jesus in his last journey to Jerusalem came up to Bethany and Bethphage on Mount of Olives, he sent two of his disciples into the nearby village to bring an ass (colt). They brought the colt and Jesus sat on it. Many spread their garments in the way and others cut down branches of the trees and spread them on the way. They that went before and they that followed cried, saying "Hosanna! Blessed is he that cometh in the name of the Lord. Blessed be his kingdom of our father David! that cometh in the name of the Lord, Hosanna in the highest!"

Jesus entered the temple in Jerusalem, looked around and as it was evening, he went with his disciples to Bethany.

Plot to Kill Jesus

According to Matthew 26:1 to 5, Mark 14: 1and 2 and Luke 22 :1 to 6, the chief priest and the elders of the people assembled in the place of high priest, whose name was Caiaphas and they plotted to arrest Jesus in some sly way and kill him. But, not during the forthcoming feast of the Unleavened Bread as it may lead to a riot among the people.

Jesus Anointed in Bethany

According to Matthew 26:6 to13, Mark 14:3 to 9 when Jesus was in the house of Simon the leper in Bethany, a woman came and anointed Jesus with a precious ointment. Some people said that it was a waste to use such costly perfume. But Jesus said she prepared his body for burial.

Judas Iscariot Agreed to Betray Jesus

According to Luke 22: 1 to 6 the chief priest and the scribes sought to kill Jesus, but they were scared of people's agitation. Then, Satan entered into Judas Iscariot, one of the disciples of Jesus, who went to the chief priest and captains and agreed to take money from them by betraying Jesus in the absence of the multitudes. From that time onwards, Judas Iscariot was seeking an opportunity to betray Jesus.

According to Matthew 26:14 and 15 Judas agreed with the chief priest to deliver Jesus for thirty pieces of silver.

The Last Supper of Jesus with His Disciples

According to Matthew 26: 17 to 30, Mark 14 :12-26, Luke 22:7 to 30, on the first day of the feast of the unleavened bread, Jesus asked his disciples to go into the city and a man would show them a large Upper Room furnished, where they should make preparations for Jesus to eat the Passover with his disciples. Jesus told his disciples that one of the twelve would betray him. Every one of the disciples began to question whether it was one of them who would betray Jesus. When Judas Iscariot asked Jesus, he said, "yes, it is you."

While they were eating supper, Jesus took the bread, gave thanks and broke it, and gave it to his disciples, saying, "Take, and eat; this is my body" Then he took the cup, gave thanks and offered it to them, saying, "Drink from it, all of you. This is my blood of the covenant, which is poured out for many." Then, they sang a hymn and went to the Mount of Olives (3kms away). Judas Iscariot went away to the high priests to tell his plan to handover Jesus that night itself.

Jesus Predicted the Denial of Peter

According to Matthew 26:31 to 35, Mark 14: 27 to 31, Luke 22:33 to 34, Jesus told his disciples after the last supper, "All shall be offended because of me this night, as it is written, that I will smite the shepherd, and the sheep shall be scattered." Peter said, "Though all men shall be offended because of thee, yet will I never be offended." But, Jesus said, "Verily, I say unto thee, that this night, before the cock crows, thou shalt deny me thrice."

Jesus Prayed in the Garden of Gethsemane

According to Matthew 26:36 to 47, Mark 14:32-42; Luke 22:39 to 51, Jesus along with his eleven disciples (the tweleth disciple, Judas Iscariot had gone away), went into the Garden of Gethsemane, on the Mount of Olives near Jerusalem. Jesus asked his disciples to sit at a place as he would go further to pray. Jesus took with him Peter and the two sons of Zebedee (John and James), and asked them to tarry at a place and watch with him. Jesus went a little further, and fell on his face and prayed saying, "O, my Father, if it be possible, let this cup pass from me, nevertheless, not as I will, but as thou wilt. "Jesus came three times to his disciples, but they were fast asleep. When he came a third time also, they were sleeping. Jesus said to them "Sleep on, now, and take your rest: Behold! the hour is at hand; and the Son of Man is betrayed into the hands of sinners. Rise, let us be going: Behold! he is at hand that doth betray me."

Jesus was Arrested in the Garden of Gethsemane

According to Matthew 26:47 to 56, Mark 14:43-52, and Luke 22:47 to 51, while Jesus was still speaking to his disciples, Judas Iscariot came with a large crowd, armed with swords and staves. Judas Iscariot came to Jesus and said, "Hail, master" and kissed him, as it was the sign given to the Roman soldiers to identify Jesus amongst his disciples. Jesus said to the multitude, "Are ye come out as against a thief with swords and staves to take me? I sat daily with you teaching in the temple, and ye laid no hold on me." They all took Jesus to the high priests. All the disciples forsook Jesus and fled, leaving Jesus alone with the crowd.

Jesus was Judged in the Sanhedrin

According to Matthew 26:75 to 68, Mark 14: 53-65, Luke 22:52 to 54, they that laid hold on Jesus and took him to Caiaphas the high priest, where all the scribes and elders were assembled. Caiaphas tried to find fault in Jesus, but could not. Caiaphas asked Jesus whether he was the Christ the Son of God. Jesus said, "yes." Caiaphas tore his clothes and said that Jesus was worthy of death, as he had spoken blasphemy. The people spat in Jesus' face and other, smote him with the palms of their hands.

Peter Denied Jesus Thrice

According to Matthew 26:69 to 75, Mark 14 :66 to 72, Luke 22:55 to 62, as Peter was sitting outside the Sanhedrin, the servant saw him and enquired whether he knew Jesus, and Peter denied it thrice and the cock crows. Peter remembered the words of Jesus, "Before the cock crows, thou shalt deny me thrice," and wept bitterly.

Judas Iscariot Hanged Himself

According to Matthew 27: 1 to 5, in the early morning, the chief priest and elders of the people took Jesus to Pontius Pilot, who after a long trial agreed with the people to crucify Jesus and release Barabbas, a notable prisoner. Then Judas, who had betrayed Jesus heard that Jesus was condemned to crucification, he repented, and brought the thirty pieces of silver to the chief priests and elders, saying, "I have sinned in that I have betrayed the innocent blood." But, they said, "What is that to us? See thou to that." Judas Iscariot threw down the thirty pieces of silver in the temple, went out and hanged himself. The chief priest took the thirty pieces of silver and felt that it was the price of blood and therefore should not be put in treasury. They purchased a potter's field with this money to bury the strangers. This field is known as the "Field of Blood" till this day.

Jesus before Pontius Pilot

According to Matthew 27:11 to 26, Mark 15:1 to 15, Luke 23:1 to 25, Pontius asked many question, but Jesus did not give any reply. Pilot couldn't find any fault in Jesus to condemn him to crucifiction. But the people were shouting, asking Pilot to crucify him and release Barabbas a noted prisoner. While Pilot was sitting in the judges seat his wife sent a message to him advising him not to do anything with this innocent man as she suffered many things in her dream, because of Jesus. Pilot felt that uproar of people was starting, and he took water and washed his hands in front of the crowd, saying, "I am innocent of this man's blood, it is your responsibility. 'The people answered "Let his blood be on us and on our children. Pilot handed over Jesus to them and released Barabbas. The people and the soldiers took Jesus into a common hall, stripped Jesus and put on him a scarlet robe, made a crown of thorns and placed it on Jesus' head, a reed in his hand to mock him as king, saying, "Hail, king of Jews." Then, they put his own clothes, and led him away to crucify him.

CRUCIFICATION OF JESUS CHRIST

Now, the readers come to the most painful part of Jesus' life on this earth and all the Christians throughout the world remember this with great sorrow, as our Lord and saviour Jesus Christ was crucified and he died on the cross.

According to Matthew 27:31 to 44, Mark:15 :20 to 32, Luke 23:26 to 43 and John 19:16 to 24, Jesus was led by the the Roman soldiers and people from "Gabbatha" (Judgment hall) to "Golgotha" (Place of skull) and heavy wooden cross was placed on the shoulders of Jesus to be carried all the way (2 kms). As they came out of Gabbatha, they met a man named Simon Cyrene and they compelled him to bear the cross. Due to the heavy weight of the cross, Jesus fell down thrice by the time he reached Golgotha (Place of skull) and the Roman soldiers whipped him to get up and continue to bear the cross. Jesus consoled the women of Jerusalem, who were following the cross by saying, "Daughters of Jerusalem, do not weep for me: weep for yourselves and your children." When they came to Golgotha, they gave him vinegar to drink mingled with gall but, Jesus tasted it and did not drink. They crucified Jesus and parted with his garments by casting lots. Two other thieves were also crucified along with Jesus, one the right hand and the other on the left. On the top of the cross it was written "THIS IS JESUS, THE KING OF THE JEWS." The passersby reviled Jesus wagging their heads, and saying, "Thou shall destroy the temple and buildest it in three day, save thyself. If thou be the Son of God, come down from the cross." Similarly, the chief priests the scribes and the elders said, "He saved others, himself he cannot save. If he be the King of Israel, let him now come down from the cross and we will believe him." One of the thieves who was crucified with Jesus also made similar remarks. But the other thief asked Jesus to remember him in Heaven.

SEVEN WORDS SPOKEN BY JESUS FROM THE CROSS

While Jesus Christ was on the cross for nearly six hours, he spoke the following seven words:-

1. **FIRST WORD:** "Father, forgive them, for they do not know what they are doing."

    This is an amazing forgiveness of Jesus Christ, though he was mocked, beaten and crucified (Luke 23: 34).

2. **SECOND WORD:** "I tell you the truth, today you will be with me in paradise"(Luke 23:43). One of the thieves who was crucified with Jesus mocked Jesus by saying, "Aren't you the Christ? Save yourself and us!" But , the other thief rebuked him, saying, "Don't you fear God? We are punished for our bad deeds, but this man has done nothing wrong." Then he said, "Jesus, remember me when you enter into your kingdom." Then, Jesus spoke the above second word.

3. **THIRD WORD:** "Dear woman, here is your son, and he said to his disciple here is your mother" (John 19:25 to 27). Near the cross, Jesus' mother her sister, Mary the wife of Clopas and Mary Magdalene were standing and crying. When Jesus saw his mother and the disciple, whom he loved standing nearby, Jesus said to his mother and the disciple the above words. From that time onwards, this disciple took her into his home.

4. **FOURTH WORD:** "Eloi, Eloi Lama Sabacthani?" which means, "My, God my God, why have

you forsaken me? (Mt. 27: 45 and 46, Mark 15:34). From the sixth hour (12:00 noon) onwards till the ninth hour (3:00p.m) there was darkness all over the land. About the ninth hour (3:00 p.m), Jesus cried out in loud voice, saying the above words.

5. FIFTH WORD: "I thirst" (John 19:28 and 29). Later on knowing that all was now completed, so that the scriptures maybe fulfilled, Jesus said the above word. A jar of wine mixed with vinegar was there. So, they soaked a sponge in it, put the sponge on a stalk of hyssop plant, and lifted it to Jesus' lips.

6. SIXTH WORD: "It is finished" (John 19:30), when Jesus had received the vinegar He said the above word, bowed his head and gave up the ghost.

7. SEVENTH WORD: "Father, into your hand I commit my spirit" (Luke: 23:44 to 47).

When Jesus said this word, he breathed his last. The centurions, seeing what happened praised God and said "Surely this was a righteous man"

Thus, all the seven words spoken by Jesus from the cross are not in one gospel, but in all the four gospels, most of them are in John's gospel.

Jesus' Body was Placed in the Rock Tomb

According to Mt. 27:57 to 66, Mark 15:43 -47, Luke 23:50 to 56 and John 19:38 to 42 a person named Joseph of Arimathaea, a secret disciple of Jesus, went to Pilot and begged for the body of Jesus, who died on the cross. Pilot commanded the body to be delivered. Joseph wrapped it in a clean linen cloth and laid it in his own new tomb, which he had hewn out in the rock and he rolled a great stone to the door of the sepulchure and departed. As it was a preparation day and the next day was Sabbath and as the rock tomb was near the place of crucification in a garden it was convenient to place Jesus' body there. All the women of Jerusalem saw the tomb. The Roman soldiers sealed the tomb with a stone and a set a watch in the nights, thinking that the disciples might come and take away the body, as Jesus said that he would rise from the dead on the third day.

Resurrection of Jesus

According to Matthew 28:1 to 20, Mark 16:1 to 20, Luke 24:1 to 49 and John Chapter 20, Chap 21:1 to 25, on the first day of the week (Sunday) very early in the morning the women took the spices they prepared for anointing Jesus' body and went to the tomb. On the way they were discussing one with another as to who would roll away the big stone from the mouth of the rock tomb. But, when they all reached the tomb, they were surprised to see that the big stone had already been rolled away. When they went inside the tomb they did not find the body of Jesus. Two men in shining clothes appeared to them when the women bowed down their heads to the ground. These men said to them, "why do you look for the living among the dead? He is not here, he has risen."

All the women went away and told the eleven disciples the things they had seen, but they did not believe the words of these women. Peter ran to the tomb and bending over it, he saw the strips of linen lying and he went away. On the same day, two men were going from Jerusalem to Emmaus (10 kms away). Jesus joined them. They were talking about the crucification of Jesus Christ. They did not realise that it was Jesus who was travelling with them. In the evening, when they reached Emmaus, Jesus acted as if he was going to another place but, they stopped him and asked him to spend the night with them. At dinner time, when all the three sat at the table, Jesus took bread, gave thanks, broke it and began to give it to the other two. Then their eyes were opened and they realized that it was Jesus. Jesus disappeared from there. The two men returned to Jerusalem and told the eleven disciples all the things they experienced.

While they were all still talking, Jesus himself stood among them, and said to them, "Peace be with you." They were amazed and thought that it was a ghost. But, Jesus showed them his hand and feet, where nails were driven during his crucification and he said, "Touch me, and see: A ghost does not have flesh and bone as you see I have. Jesus asked them whether they had anything to eat. They gave him a piece of broiled fish, which Jesus took and ate it in their presence.

In John 21:15 to 17 Jesus asked Simon Peter whether he loved him. Jesus asked three times and Peter was a little grieved. Then Jesus said to Peter, "Feed my sheep."

Ascension of Jesus Christ into Heaven

According to Luke 24:50 to 53 Jesus spoke to his disciples saying "Behold, I send the promise of my Father upon you: but tarry ye in the city of Jerusalem, until ye be endued with power from on high." Jesus led his eleven disciples out as far as to Bethany (3 kms away) and he lifted up his hands and blessed them. As he was blessing them, he was parted from them and carried up into heaven. The disciples were continually in the temple, praising and blessing God.

15.

Fourteen Stations of the Cross (Via - Dolorosa)

In Jesus' days "Gabbatha" (Judgment Hall), where Pontius Pilot judged Jesus Christ was within the city of Jerusalem and "Golgotha "(Place of skull), where Jesus Christ was crucified was outside the city walls of Jerusalem. As the city of Jerusalem expanded all these years, now Golgotha is also in the old city of Jerusalem. The distance between Gabbatha and Golgotha is about 1.5 kilometers. So Jesus Christ had to carry the heavy wooden cross on his shoulder for a distance of 1.5kms except for a short while when the cross was carried by Simon Cyrene. Due to the heavy weight of the cross, Jesus fell three times on this route but the Roman soldiers whipped him to rise up and continue to bear the cross.

As Jesus Christ carried the cross along this 1.5 kms route from Gabbatha to Golgotha, the events that took place from the time he took the cross on his shoulders till he died on the cross and his body placed in the rock tomb are considered as fourteen events and they are called by Roman Catholic Christians as fourteen stations of the Cross. From the years 326 A.D when Emperor Constantine of Rome and his mother, Queen Helena visited Jerusalem after they were converted as Christian and started constructing many churches in Jerusalem (Churches of the Holy Sepulchure), Bethlehem (Church of

Nativity) the terms like "Via-Dolorosa" and other terms were introduced.

The term "Via-Dolorosa" is an Italian term. "Via means way and Dolorosa" means "sorrow". Thus, "Via Dolorosa means "way of sorrow." Some times, this is also known as way of the cross, because this is the way along which, Jesus Christ carried the cross on his shoulders from Gabbatha to Golgotha.

The following plan shows the fourteen stations of the Cross. These fourteen stations are now accommodated in different chapels', churches, monasteries etc. The fourteen stations in this plan are indicated by Roman letter and the route is shown in dots. The name of different chapels', churches and monasteries in which the fourteen stations are now accommodated are also shown in the plan.

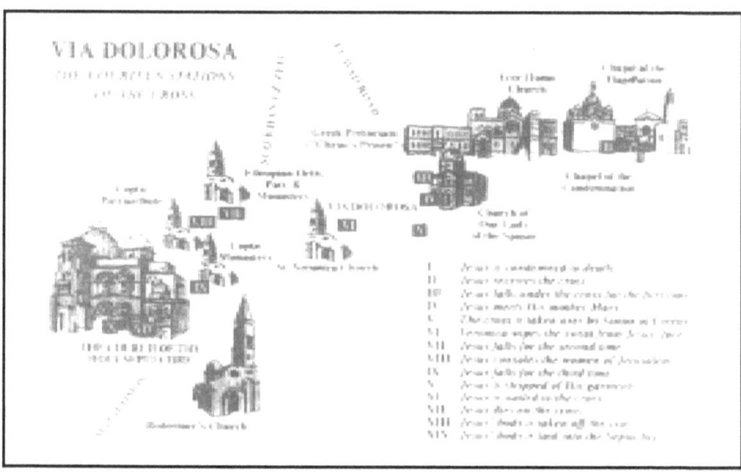

IST STATION : JESUS IS CONDEMNED TO DEATH

This station is now accommodated in the courtyard of Al-Omariya School. Jesus Christ was taken away by the Roman soldiers from the Court of Pontius Pilot (Gabbatha). Pontius Pilot washed his hand in a basin of water, saying, "I am innocent of this man's blood."

IIND STATION: JESUS RECEIVED THE CROSS ON HIS SHOULDERS

This station is now in the Franciscon Chapel of Flagellation and the Chapel of Condemnation. The Roman soldiers placed the cross on Jesus' shoulders to carry from Gabbatha to Golgotha which was about 1.5 kms.

IIIRD STATION: JESUS FELL UNDER THE CROSS FOR THE FIRST TIME

This station is now accomodated in the American Catholic Chapel. Due to the heavy weight of the cross, Jesus fell for the first time. Roman soldiers whipped him to rise up and continue to bear the cross. Some soldiers even pulled up Jesus to stand again.

IVTH STATION: JESUS MET HIS MOTHER, MARY STANDING BY

This station is now in the Armenian Church of our Lady Spasm. As Jesus Christ was going along the way from Gabbatha to Golgotha some women of Jerusalem including Mary the mother of Jesus were following him. Jesus looked at his mother and consoled her.

V^{TH} STATION: CROSS IS TAKEN OVER BY SIMON CYRENE

This station is now in Fraciscon Chapel. As Jesus Christ fell with the weight of the cross, the Roman soldier asked Simon Cyrene, who was passing by, to bear the cross for some time.

VITH STATION: VERONICA WIPED THE SWEAT FROM JESUS' FACE

This particular event is not mentioned in the Holy Bible. But the Roman Catholic Christians believe that a sister by the name Veronica, took out her head scarf and wiped that sweat from Jesus' face. It is also believed that the imprint of Jesus's face was left on the scarf. This scarf is now preserved in St. Peter' Church in Rome (Italy). It is also believed that all the present day pictures of Jesus are taken from this imprint on the scarf.

VII ᵀᴴ STATION: JESUS FELL FOR THE SECOND TIME

This station is now in two chapels, connected together. The Roman soldier pulled up Jesus to bear the cross.

VIIIᵀᴴ STATION: JESUS CONSOLED THE WOMEN OF JERUSALEM

As Jesus Christ was going with the heavy cross on his shoulders from Gabbath to Golgotha, a group of women from Jerusalem knew Jesus well , were sitting at a place on this route. When Jesus came to them, he looked at them and consoled them by saying, "Daughters of Jerusalem, weep not for me but weep for yourself and your children" (Luke 23:28).

XIᵀᴴ STATION: JESUS FELL FOR THE THIRD TIME

This station is now shown on one of the columns of the Coptic Church. Once again the Roman soldiers whipped Jesus and pulled him up to stand and carry the cross.

Xᵀᴴ STATION: JESUS IS STRIPPED OFF HIS GARMENT

When Jesus Christ arrived at Golgotha with the cross on his shoulders, the Roman soldiers parted with his garment by casting lots (Mt. 27:35 and Mark 15:22 to 24).

XIᵀᴴ STATION :JESUS IS NAILED TO THE CROSS

When Jesus arrived at Golgotha the Roman soldiers laid the cross on the ground, made Jesus stretch himself on it with his hands wide open and they drove large metal nails into his hands and feet (Luke 23:33).

His mother, Mary was watching this most horrible sight with great sorrow and crying alongwith other women of Jerusalem.

XII*TH* STATION: JESUS DIED ON THE CROSS

At the ninth hour (3:00 p.m), Jesus cried with a loud voice and gave up his spirit (Mark 15 :34 to 37). All the women of Jerusalem were at the cross, as Jesus died.

XIII*TH* STATION : JESUS'S BODY WAS TAKEN OFF THE CROSS

When Jesus died on the cross, the Roman soldiers climbed up the cross with the help of ladders and took down the dead body of Jesus from the cross and it was laid in the lap of his mother, Mary. This is another most pathetic scene of Mary holding the dead body of her son.

XIV*TH* STATION: JESUS' DEAD BODY WAS LAID IN THE SEPULCHURE

A rich man Joseph of Arimath and a secret disciple of Jesus Christ went to Pontius Pilot in the evening and begged for the body of Jesus Christ. Pilot commanded the body to be delivered to Joseph. Then Joseph wrapped the Body of Jesus in clean linen and placed it in a rock tomb made for him and his family members. Its was in a garden near Golgotha. He rolled a big stone to the mouth of the tomb and went away. The women of Jerusalem saw this tomb (Mt. 27:57 to 60 and Mark 15:46 and 47).

Now a days, the Protestant Christians believe that the place of skull (Golgotha) and the nearby rock tomb both of which are in garden as mentioned in the Holy Bible are the correct location of Jesus crucification. This is now known as "Garden Tomb" in Jerusalem. On the otherhand, the Roman Catholic Christians believe that these two spots are in the Church of Holy Sepulchure built by Emperor Constantine of Rome and his mother, Queen Helena. In fact, the Emperor accommodated the last five stations (stations X to XIV) of via - Dolorosa within this huge Church. The first nine stations are accomodated in different chapels, churches and monasteries, as explained earlier.

Via Dolorosa is considered to be the most holy spot in Jerusalem. So, no pilgrim misses to walk along Via Dolorosa, though it is 1.5 kms long. It is firmly believed by all pilgrims that by walking along Via Dolorosa one might be walking in the foot steps of Jesus Christ, while he was carrying the cross from Gabbatha to Golgotha. Now a days many pilgrims, carry wooden cross on their shoulder one after the other by rotation and a big procession of other pilgrims follow and go along the entire route of Via Doloroso. This is usually done on Friday, as Jesus Christ was crucified on Friday. It is a sight to see that even the crippled in wheel chairs and lame walk all the way with great belief.

16.

Blessings

May our Lord Savior JESUS CHRIST bless all the Sunday schools and the Sunday School staff, and all the children, so that the children may learn more about the Holy Bible from their young age and propogate its contents to all children, from generation to generation.

Similarly, May our Lord and Saviour JESUS CHRIST bless all the women's fellowships so that, they may train the children in a God fearing manner and the women's fellowship may act as organizations to bring about an overall development of entire community around them.

May our Lord and Saviour JESUS CHRIST
bless all the readers of this book.

| Ark of Covenant | Altar on festival days |

Members of Women's Fellowship in front of the Holy Cross Cathedral, Nandyal (A.P.) Rt. Rev. P.J. Lawrence, Bishop of Nandyal and his wife and Rev. Dr. Gnanakan Raj, Vicar seated.